THE CIVIL WAR AT
PERRYVILLE

THE CIVIL WAR AT
PERRYVILLE

BATTLING FOR THE BLUEGRASS

CHRISTOPHER L. KOLAKOWSKI

Charleston   London

THE
History
PRESS

Published by The History Press
Charleston, SC 29403
www.historypress.net

Copyright © 2009 by Christopher L. Kolakowski
All rights reserved

First published 2009
Second printing 2011
Third printing 2011
Fourth printing 2011

Manufactured in the United States

ISBN 978.1.59629.672.5

Library of Congress Cataloging-in-Publication Data

Kolakowski, Christopher L.
The Civil War at Perryville : battling for the Bluegrass / Christopher L. Kolakowski.
p. cm.
Includes bibliographical references and index.
ISBN 978-1-59629-672-5 (alk. paper)
1. Perryville, Battle of, Perryville, Ky., 1862. 2. Kentucky--History--Civil War,
1861-1865--Campaigns. 3. United States--History--Civil War, 1861-1865--Campaigns.
I. Title.
E474.39.K65 2009
973.7'33--dc22
2009026260

For my parents

CONTENTS

ACKNOWLEDGEMENTS

I first came to Perryville in August 2005 as part of a Civil War conference. I had always been vaguely aware that a major battle had occurred there, but by no means was overly familiar with it. The pristine fields and woods, very indicative of how it looked in 1862, made quite an impression on me. By happenstance, I got the opportunity to work there a few months later, and in November 2005 became executive director of the Perryville Enhancement Project, a public-private partnership charged with preserving and interpreting the Perryville Battlefield and related sites. The three years I spent in Perryville were very rewarding, and I came to appreciate this battle and site for what it truly is. Perryville will always be a special place for me.

Although my name appears on the cover of this book, this work would not have been possible without the help of others. First and foremost, thanks go to my former colleagues and partners at Perryville: Kurt Holman, Joan House, Chad Greene, Don Kelly, Rich Stallings, Nancy Ross-Stallings, Robert Preston, Darrell Young and Harold Edwards. They all contributed in ways large and small to my understanding of Kentucky's largest battle and I cannot forget it. Kurt is a walking encyclopedia on the battle, and his enthusiastic support was key to this project. He is a true asset to that site.

Others who contributed to this project include Nicky Hughes of the Frankfort City Museum, Phil Seyfrit of the Richmond Battlefield Park, Tom Fugate, Tres Seymour of the Battle for the Bridge Historic Preserve in Munfordville, Homer Musselman, Steve Garvey and Lynne Grant, Kirk Jenkins, Mike Formichella, Micah Morris, Duncan Granger, Betty Jane Gorin, Ken Noe of Auburn University, Dr. Robert Cameron of Fort Knox,

ACKNOWLEDGEMENTS

Stuart Sanders and Don Rightmyer of the Kentucky Historical Society and the Kentucky Humanities Council. Great thanks are also due to Jim Cass, John Strojan and M.C. Edwards of the Camp Wildcat Preservation Foundation, and Paul Rominger, Bob Moody and Ed Ford of the Battle of Richmond Association. John Walsh's excellent maps added immensely to this work. I also would like to thank The History Press and my editor, John Wilkinson, who was a pleasure to work with and patient with a first-time book author. Any and all errors in this work are mine alone.

Active preservation movements are working to preserve and interpret the key sites associated with the 1862 Kentucky Campaign. For more information and links, please visit www.kycivilwar.org.

INTRODUCTION

The Commonwealth of Kentucky has a rich military tradition dating back to before its founding in 1792. Rangers from the Kentucky counties of Virginia engaged a British and native force at Blue Licks in 1782, one of the last American battles during the War for Independence. Kentucky riflemen formed elite units in General Andrew Jackson's army during the War of 1812, and the Kentucky Militia played a decisive part in the victory at New Orleans in January 1815. In every subsequent war this country has waged, Kentucky units and leaders have played an important role; the state's military history is emblazoned with names like Mexico, the Argonne, Bataan and Corregidor, the Ia Drang Valley and Iraq.

Kentucky's military story is dominated by the Civil War period. U.S. president Abraham Lincoln and his counterpart, Jefferson Davis, were each native Kentuckians, and both men realized the importance of possessing the Bluegrass State on their side. Kentucky was a slave state but joined the Union in 1861 after an abortive attempt at neutrality. The men of Kentucky divided their loyalties also: 100,000 fought for the United States, while 40,000 carried arms for the Confederacy. Prominent politicians and generals on both sides came from the state.

The Civil War was also the last time the Bluegrass State suffered invasion. Union and Confederate armies raced for possession of the state in 1861, a race won by the Union. Repeated Confederate cavalry raids inflamed Kentucky's countryside for the entire war. But the largest and most important invasion of the state came in 1862, as the Confederacy attempted one last time to turn Kentucky to the Southern cause. For ten weeks in the late summer and fall of 1862, the fate of the Bluegrass State hung in the balance as Confederate armies surged into Kentucky and Union armies maneuvered to prevent them from taking control. The issue was decided forever on October 8, 1862, at Perryville, a crossroads town in the center of the state, where two major armies clashed and the dream of a Confederate Kentucky suffered a mortal blow. The Bluegrass State remained in the Union camp for the rest of the war.

The 1862 Kentucky Campaign was the largest and bloodiest military operation ever mounted in Kentucky. By the time it was over, the contending armies had covered almost all of the central and eastern parts of the state, from the Tennessee border in the south to the Ohio River in the north. The campaign produced Kentucky's largest and bloodiest battle at Perryville, the state's second-largest battle at Richmond and one of the largest U.S. surrenders of the war at Munfordville. These dramatic events together represent the High Water Mark of the Confederacy in the West. In many ways, both the fate of Kentucky and the fate of the United States rested on the outcome of the campaign and Battle of Perryville.

CHAPTER 1

THE SIREN SONG OF KENTUCKY

C hattanooga, Tennessee, shimmered in the summer heat on the last day of July 1862. The town and its surrounding ridges swarmed with Confederate troops as an army of thirty thousand men arrived by train and crowded in and around the town of two thousand residents. The buzz of activity broke through the oppressive temperatures.

The nexus of all this military commotion was the downtown hotel that served as headquarters for the Army of the Mississippi, as this incoming force was known. In an upstairs room, two Confederate generals were meeting that day to discuss options and plans. Seen side by side, the two men offered an interesting contrast—one tall and erect of bearing, while the other was shorter and more dour.[1]

The taller officer was Major General Edmund Kirby Smith, who commanded the Department of East Tennessee with headquarters in Knoxville. Kirby Smith was a native Floridian who brought a distinguished record to this meeting. At age seventeen, he had entered West Point and graduated in 1845 in the middle of his class. A veteran of the Mexican War, where he won two brevet promotions for bravery, he compiled a solid record as an Indian fighter in the 1850s. In 1861, he resigned from the U.S. Army and followed his native state into the Confederacy. At the First Battle of Manassas in July 1861, Kirby Smith's brigade arrived last on the field and launched a smashing counterattack that started the Federal rout. Wounded in the action, he emerged, along with Brigadier General Thomas J. "Stonewall" Jackson, as a principal hero of the battle. He had come to East Tennessee in February 1862 with the dual mission of defending the area

Edmund Kirby Smith. *Madison County Historic Sites.*

and holding down the restive pro-Union population. The job in Knoxville was an important but less glamorous post, especially compared to some of his contemporaries' commands. An egocentric and vain man, by July Kirby Smith was looking for an opportunity to regain the glory of Manassas.[2]

Kirby Smith had traveled down from Knoxville to meet his counterpart, a man he later described to his wife as "a grim old fellow, but a true soldier." General Braxton Bragg was commander of the Army of the Mississippi. Bragg hailed from a North Carolina family of social outcasts; some question exists as to whether he was born while his mother was in jail or shortly after she completed her sentence. Bragg's father pushed him into a military career, so the future general graduated from West Point in 1837 and spent the next eighteen years in the U.S. Army, seeing action against the Seminoles in Florida and in the Mexican War. His achievements at the Battle of Buena

The Siren Song of Kentucky

Braxton Bragg. *Perryville Battlefield State Historic Site.*

Vista in 1847 made him a national hero despite notable blots on his record that included two court-martials, an attempted assassination attempt by his subordinates and a reputation for extreme contentiousness. Bragg cast his lot with the Confederacy in 1861, and by 1862 was known as a tough drillmaster but a solid subordinate officer. He took command of the Army of Mississippi in mid-June, just six weeks before this meeting with Kirby Smith. Despite his shorter tenure in top command, Bragg was the senior of the two generals.[3]

As the two men pored over their maps, a grim situation presented itself. For the past eight months, Federal armies had won an unbroken string of victories in the West. Now their forces sprawled all over most of Tennessee, northern Mississippi and northern Alabama. Much of this damage had been accomplished by two major Federal armies. Major General Ulysses S. Grant's Army of the Tennessee was operating between Nashville and Memphis, while Major General Don Carlos Buell's Army of the Ohio occupied much of middle Tennessee between Nashville and the Cumberland Plateau outside Chattanooga. At that moment, Buell's Yankees were slowly advancing toward Chattanooga, gateway to Atlanta and the Southern heartland. The war in the West appeared to be nearing a major turning point.[4]

Don Carlos Buell. *Perryville Battlefield State Historic Site.*

The path of war in the Western Theater had been full of dramatic twists and turns up to this point. In many of the shifts, the key had been Kentucky. When North and South divided in the spring of 1861, Kentucky found itself torn between a pro-Union legislature and a pro-secession governor. A compromise declared Kentucky neutral, effectively creating a buffer zone between the Union and the Confederacy stretching from the Appalachian Mountains to the Mississippi River. Union armies gathered north of the Ohio River, while in Tennessee Confederate forces coalesced around Nashville and northern border cities. Neither side wanted to provoke Kentucky into joining the other camp. Tension rose during the summer of 1861 as each side waited for the other to tip the balance.

Coincidentally, both U.S. president Abraham Lincoln and Confederate president Jefferson Davis were native Kentuckians. Davis had been born near Hopkinsville in June 1808, while Lincoln followed the next February about one hundred miles east at Hodgenville. Each man knew that his native state would confer great advantages to whichever side controlled it.

The Siren Song of Kentucky

Kentucky offered a good pool of recruits for an army, while rich farmland could supply plentiful foodstuffs. Armies in the 1860s depended on horses and mules to operate, and the central Bluegrass region was one of the best sources of horseflesh in North America. Geographically, Kentucky touched all of the important rivers for the Union war effort: the Ohio, the Tennessee, the Mississippi and the Cumberland. These watercourses offered good invasion and supply routes for U.S. forces, while the Confederates could use them as effective obstacles to any Union advance. Lincoln summed up the state's importance when he wrote, "I think to lose Kentucky is nearly the same as to lose the whole game."[5]

The delicate balance in the West was upset in early September 1861 when a Confederate force under General Leonidas Polk moved into Kentucky and captured the town of Columbus on the Mississippi River. This act, spurred by erroneous reports of Federal troops in Paducah, set in motion a race for the state as both sides moved to seize territory. The Kentucky General

Leonidas Polk. *Perryville Battlefield State Historic Site.*

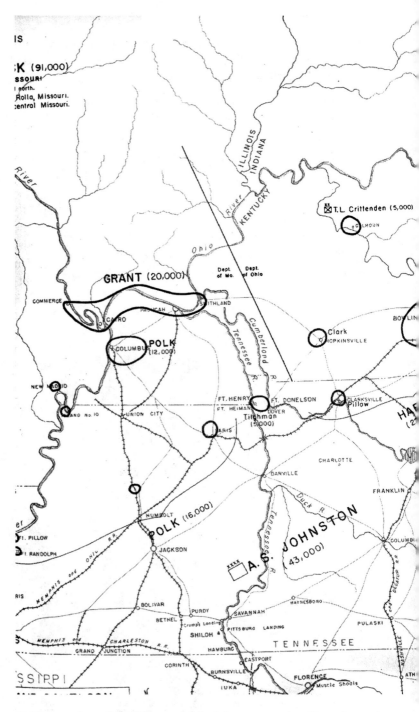

Confederate forces from Tennessee begin their movement into Kentucky.
West Point Atlas of American Wars, author's collection.

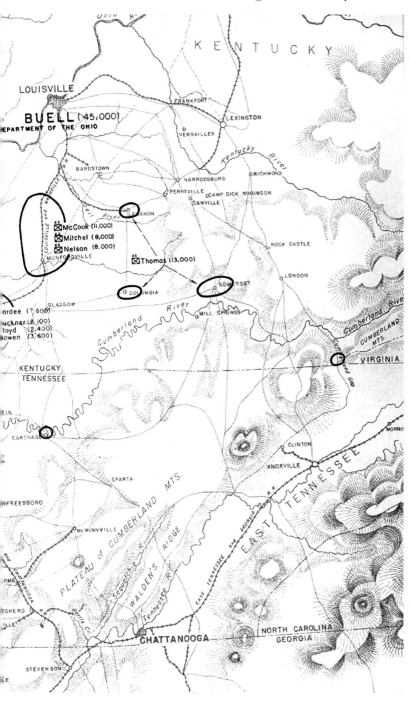

Assembly in Frankfort voted to remain loyal to the United States, while in late October a separate convention in Russellville created a provisional government and passed an ordinance of secession. Kentucky was admitted into the Confederate States of America. The onset of winter found the Confederates in possession of the southern third of the state, while the rest had fallen into Union hands.

Both sides spent the winter consolidating their positions and preparing for a major campaign in 1862. Confederate forces, now commanded by Kentucky-born general Albert Sidney Johnston, set up a thin defensive line across southern Kentucky. One of the major weaknesses of Johnston's position was that the Tennessee and Cumberland Rivers led southward through his defenses; any determined thrust by Federal troops along those waterways could unhinge his whole line.

Buell's army tested the Confederate line in January, smashing the eastern flank in the Battle of Mill Springs, near Somerset. Grant's force at Paducah next moved south into Tennessee, and in February captured Forts Henry and Donelson and sixteen thousand men. At a stroke, Johnston's army in Kentucky was outflanked and its lines of communication to Nashville threatened with rupture. Grant moved up the Tennessee River to Pittsburg Landing near the Mississippi border, while Buell surged toward Nashville.[6]

Faced with the prospect of a defeat in detail, Johnston was forced to retreat. He abandoned Nashville and decided to concentrate his scattered commands at Corinth, Mississippi, an easy march from Grant's camp. Polk joined him in Corinth, as did reinforcements under Braxton Bragg from Pensacola. At dawn on April 6, Johnston attacked Grant at Pittsburg Landing. The battle lasted all day and came excruciatingly close to driving Grant's army into the river, but at the cost of Johnston's life. Much of Buell's army arrived that evening and crossed the river, making good Grant's losses from the day's fighting. The combined Federal forces counterattacked the next day and drove the Confederates (now under General P.G.T. Beauregard) from the field in disorder. Thus ended the Battle of Pittsburg Landing, or Shiloh, as the Confederates called it—the first truly great battle of the Civil War.[7]

After Shiloh, both sides reorganized. Beauregard licked his wounds in Corinth, while the Federal armies prepared to follow up their victory. Major General Henry W. Halleck, the Federal supreme commander in the West,

The Siren Song of Kentucky

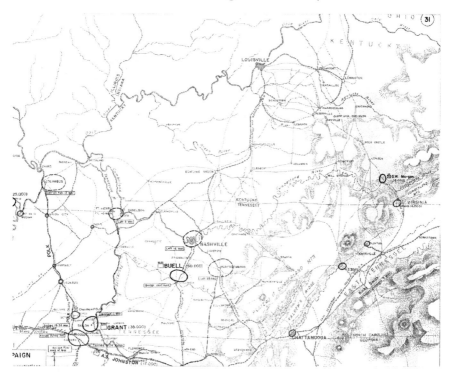

The Western Theater on the eve of the Battle of Shiloh. West Point Atlas of American Wars, *author's collection.*

came to Pittsburg Landing and assumed command of both Grant's and Buell's armies. In late April, Halleck's force, now numbering 100,000 men, moved south on a methodical advance toward Corinth. The Union troops averaged one mile of progress per day and after a month finally arrived at Corinth to find it deserted. Beauregard had retreated south to Tupelo without a fight.

Instead of pursuing his enemy to destruction, Halleck now divided his forces in an effort to capture territory. In June, Grant's army shifted west and northwest to secure Memphis and West Tennessee, while Buell's Army of the Ohio was ordered eastward from Corinth toward the critical rail junction of Chattanooga. If Buell captured that city, he would hold the gateway to the Deep South and be just one hundred miles from Atlanta.[8]

Grant met with swift success in West Tennessee, but Buell's movement progressed slowly due to supply problems. The Federals had to depend on one railroad that was easily cut by Confederate marauders. The enemy had also destroyed much of its infrastructure and rolling stock, including two large bridges over the Tennessee River. The Army of the Ohio was forced to rebuild as it marched in the heat of a Mississippi and Alabama summer. Although a small detachment of Buell's army had shelled Chattanooga, his main body was only just approaching the city by late July. It had taken his men six weeks to travel from Corinth to the Cumberland Plateau.[9]

The Confederates perceived the threat to Chattanooga and had not been idle. Bragg replaced Beauregard after the latter took ill, and one of the first messages he received was a plea for help from Kirby Smith in East Tennessee. In addition to Buell's advance to the south, Kirby Smith also was eyeing nine thousand Federals under Brigadier General George Morgan, who had occupied Cumberland Gap and appeared poised to strike toward Knoxville. East Tennessee faced threats from both the north and southwest, and a Federal pincer movement faced a high probability of success. Bragg responded to Kirby Smith's concerns and moved his entire army by rail to Chattanooga in late July. Thus, Bragg and Kirby Smith came face to face on July 31 to plan their next move.[10]

Several options presented themselves. Both men rejected a defensive strategy and decided to take the initiative. Bragg proposed a campaign to retake Nashville. In addition to being the key to middle Tennessee, Nashville was also the only Confederate capital city in Union hands at that point in the war; a victory there would compare favorably in prestige to Robert E. Lee's Confederate triumphs in Virginia outside Richmond. Kirby Smith agreed to make an offensive and pressed for a supporting operation against Cumberland Gap as a necessary prerequisite to the Nashville movement.

After much discussion, both men agreed that Kirby Smith would first advance against the gap with twenty-one thousand men, including two brigades from Bragg's army. Once Cumberland Gap was recaptured, both armies would mount a coordinated operation against Nashville. The offensive would start in the middle of August. President Davis assented to this plan but left it to the two commanders to cooperate as independent armies; only when both forces came together on the field would Bragg assume command as senior officer.[11]

Kirby Smith returned to Knoxville and soon began having second thoughts about the agreement. What historian Kenneth Noe called "Kentucky's siren song of glory" began to lure him. For some time, exiled Kentucky politicians had been pushing for a renewed offensive into the Bluegrass State, claiming that the population was really on the side of the Confederacy. Kentucky native John Hunt Morgan had led a small cavalry command toward Lexington in July and reported to Kirby Smith that "I am here with a force sufficient to hold the country outside Lexington and Frankfort. These places are garrisoned chiefly by [half-trained] Home Guard...The whole country can be secured, and 25,000 or 30,000 men will join you at once."[12]

The call of Central Kentucky became more alluring as Kirby Smith considered what it would take to reduce George Morgan's well-supplied garrison of nine thousand at Cumberland Gap. The Confederate plan depended on speed and needed to avoid a long siege, but the Federal garrison at Cumberland Gap was too strong to be taken quickly. The prospect of rich supplies and recruits in Central Kentucky also beckoned. Lexington itself was a splendid prize: the home of John C. Breckinridge, Mary Todd Lincoln and the late Henry Clay, the city was known as the "Athens of the West." Kirby Smith wrote Bragg on August 9:

> *I understand General Morgan has at Cumberland Gap nearly a month's supply of provisions. If this be true the reduction of the place would be a matter of more time than I presume you are willing I should take. As my move direct to Lexington, Ky., would effectually invest Morgan, and would be attended with other most brilliant results in my judgment, I suggest my being allowed to take that course, if I find the speedy reduction of the Gap an impracticable thing.*

Bragg was also waffling on a Nashville expedition, and he replied the next day that his "inclination is now for" Lexington as a destination, and closed with the wish that "we may all unite in Ohio." The Confederate objective had suddenly shifted from Tennessee to Kentucky.[13]

Bragg's concurrence elated Kirby Smith, who quickly made final preparations for a campaign northward. One of the intimations his men received of their destination was that the East Tennessee forces were renamed the Army of Kentucky. On August 14, 1862, Kirby Smith and his army of twenty-one thousand men left Knoxville and headed north into the mountains. The Kentucky Campaign was underway.

CHAPTER 2

THE CONFEDERATES
MOVE NORTH

The first intimation that George Morgan at Cumberland Gap received that the Confederates were after him came when his outlying pickets reported increased skirmishing in the middle of August. An accomplished diplomat and Mexican War veteran, the forty-two-year-old Morgan had been at the gap with his command since June. He was a comrade of Kirby Smith from the Mexican War and West Point. Much of the Federal garrison (known formally as the 7th Division of the Department of the Ohio) was made up of East Tennessee Union regiments who were anxious to liberate their homes. As pressure from the Confederates mounted, George Morgan drew in his pickets and foragers and awaited his old friend's next move.[14]

The Army of Kentucky entered the Bluegrass State via Rogers's Gap on August 16. Kirby Smith took with him four divisions of unequal size. Virginian Carter Stevenson commanded the 1st Division of nine thousand men, by far the largest in the army. Another Virginian, Henry Heth, led the 2nd Division of six thousand men. The 3rd Division belonged to Brigadier General Thomas W. Churchill of Texas, temporarily commanding in place of Major General John McCown, who had been left behind to command East Tennessee during Kirby Smith's absence. The Army of Kentucky's 4th Division was a provisional command of two brigades on loan from Bragg's army; its commander was a rising star named Patrick R. Cleburne, a native Irishman who had settled in Arkansas before the war. The 3rd and 4th Divisions numbered about three thousand men each. Colonel John Scott's one thousand cavalrymen rounded out the army.[15]

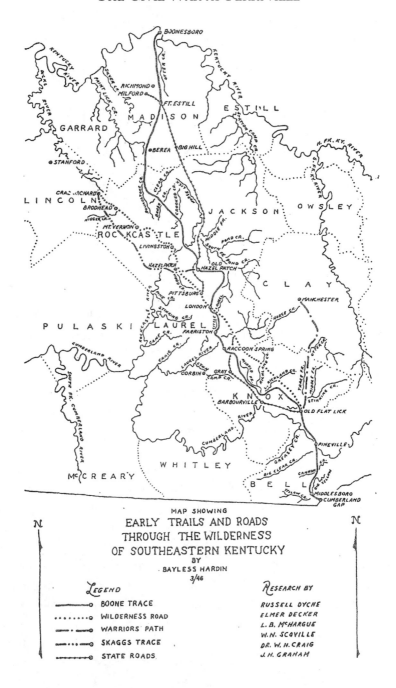

MAP SHOWING
EARLY TRAILS AND ROADS
THROUGH THE WILDERNESS
OF SOUTHEASTERN KENTUCKY
BY
BAYLESS HARDIN
3/46

The Wilderness Road was a key corridor for both armies in the campaign. North of Old Hazel Patch, the Old State Road led north toward Richmond and Lexington. Middlesboro did not exist during the time of the Civil War. *Camp Wildcat Preservation Foundation.*

The Confederates Move North

The immediate Confederate objective was simple: cut George Morgan's supply lines back to Lexington and force him to retreat or starve. The Federal supply line stretched northwest from Cumberland Gap via the Old Wilderness Road to just north of London and then turned north on the Old State Road to Richmond and Lexington. The roads themselves were in poor condition and forage was difficult to find in the mountains, so the 7th Division depended on the wagon trains that shuttled back and forth along these highways. George Morgan had scattered detachments from the 7th Kentucky Cavalry and the 3rd East Tennessee Infantry at key places along the way to protect his lifeline.[16]

Kirby Smith detached Stevenson's division to approach the gap from the south while the other three divisions moved northwest toward Barbourville and London. Federal detachments at both places put up strong fights, but superior Confederate numbers carried the day. By August 20, George Morgan's 7th Division was isolated in Cumberland Gap and pinned by Stevenson's men. As Kirby Smith's infantry consolidated and chased pro-Union bushwhackers, Colonel Scott's cavalry ranged north along the Old State Road and routed some raw Kentucky cavalrymen at Big Hill on August 23. The Confederate troopers camped near Richmond that night. The next morning, Scott retired south and reported what he had found. The way to Lexington appeared open.[17]

The news of Kirby Smith's appearance in Kentucky electrified the Union command. His presence in Barbourville meant that the largest Union force in the state east of the Tennessee River was now cut off in Cumberland Gap. Aside from some raw cavalry, the only other organized Federal unit in Kirby Smith's path was the 18th Kentucky Infantry along the railroad between Lexington and Cincinnati. Brigadier General Jeremiah Boyle, the state's military commander, frantically appealed to higher authorities as soon as Confederate intentions became clear. Reinforcements, mostly new recruits only just mustered into service, began streaming south from Indiana and Ohio. General Halleck, now general in chief in Washington, realized the danger and reorganized the Federal command structure by placing Major General Horatio Wright in command over a reorganized Department of the Ohio. By the time Scott neared Richmond on August 23, a Federal force had begun to coalesce at Lexington. Within a few days, it would grow to number eight thousand men.[18]

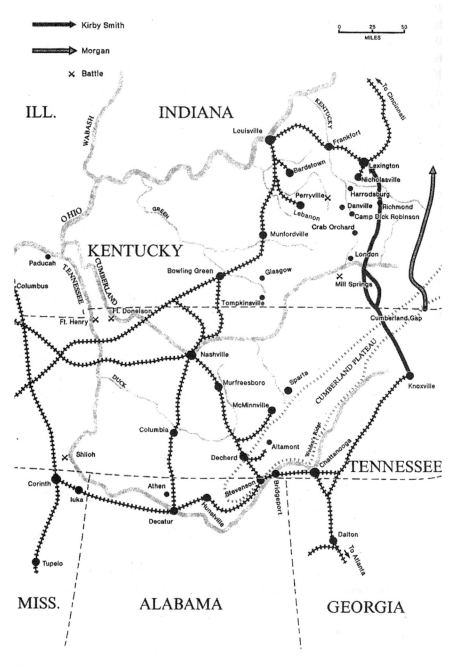

Kirby Smith's route into Kentucky. *Courtesy John P. Walsh Jr.*

The Confederates Move North

This new Union command was styled the Army of Kentucky, and it was destined to have a short and turbulent career. Its first commander was Major General Lew Wallace, who was languishing in Indiana in disgrace after failures at Shiloh. Wallace organized the defenses around Lexington and proposed to make a stand along the rugged Kentucky River Valley south of the city. That part of the river could only be crossed at three places, and the terrain favored the defenders. Wallace was assisted by the fiery Kentucky-born Major General Cassius Marcellus Clay, who happened to be in the area on a fact-finding mission from Lincoln. A violent pro-abolitionist, Clay had been Lincoln's ambassador to Russia in 1861; as a newspaper editor before the war, he had been described as "meaner than the autocrats of hell." Clay's local knowledge was a valuable asset, for his estate stood just south of the river near Richmond. Both men agreed that the Kentucky River was the place to give battle.[19]

In response to Boyle's pleas for help, Buell detached several generals and sent them north to help organize the defense of Kentucky. The highest-ranking of them was Major General William Nelson. A Kentucky native, Nelson had served as an officer in the U.S. Navy before the war. He was a very large man who weighed over three hundred pounds and was known

Charles Cruft. *Madison County Historic Sites.*

Mahlon Manson. *Madison County Historic Sites.*

as "Bull" because of his direct and aggressive temperament. In 1861, he had recruited and trained some of the first Kentucky Federal units and later commanded a division at Shiloh with some success. Nelson brought two of his subordinates with him: Brigadier Generals Charles Cruft and Mahlon Manson, both Indianans.[20]

Nelson and his party arrived in Louisville on August 20 and found pandemonium. After quarreling with Wright over command responsibilities, Nelson rode to Lexington and sent Wallace packing north. Clay did not last much longer with the Bull, despite his local knowledge; the two men were too alike in personality to get along. Nelson organized the collected troops into an army. He gave Cruft and Manson each an infantry brigade and turned the Army of Kentucky's cavalry over to Kentucky-born brigadier general James S. Jackson. Aggressively, the Bull ordered his infantry to Richmond under Manson as senior officer. The cavalry went southwest to Lancaster to guard roads and the vital depot at Camp Dick Robinson.[21]

While the Federal command buzzed with frantic preparation, at Barbourville, Kirby Smith plotted his next move. In his exultant mood he began to see himself in world-historical terms, comparable to generals like Hannibal, Caesar or Napoleon. Kirby Smith wrote his wife that his men had already accomplished "a feat rivaling the passage of the Alps." In another letter he indulged his ego further, this time casting himself in the role of Moses:

> *I have prayed for assistance and counsel from on high, and trust God will direct me on the path of victory and success...I have too much confidence in the justness and goodness of God to believe he will let us fail—and but think that like the Egyptians of old He has hardened [Federal] hearts & blinded their eyes only to make their destruction more complete.*

Sensing a great prize within his grasp, Kirby Smith made his decision. Leaving Stevenson at Cumberland Gap and Heth at Barbourville, the rest of the army set its sights on Richmond and Lexington. In the middle of oppressive heat and drought, on August 25 the Confederate Army of Kentucky again took to the road.[22]

This mid-nineteenth-century postcard view of the Wilderness Road gives some idea of its ruggedness. *Courtesy M.C. Edwards.*

In Lexington, Nelson received word from his cavalry that the Confederates were moving. Unfortunately, their direction was not clear until late on August 29, when John Scott's Confederate cavalry came over Big Hill and drove back Manson's advanced outposts. When Manson reported this encounter to Nelson late that night, the Bull ordered all infantry to move north of the Kentucky River and set off to personally reconnoiter Jackson's front.[23]

Meanwhile, Kirby Smith's vanguard spent the night of August 29 at Bobtown, about six miles south of Richmond. His army had moved fifty miles in four days over tough mountain terrain and suffered much from the heat and poor roads. The general's exultant mood continued, and he ordered General Cleburne, whose 4th Division led the infantry, to move northward at first light.[24]

Six miles north in Richmond, Mahlon Manson believed he was facing merely a small force of cavalry. Although he commanded seven thousand infantry in and around the city, he was painfully aware that most of them had less than a month of service and would have problems battling Confederate veterans. Despite this inexperience, Manson felt confident that his troops could handle Confederate cavalry. He ordered his brigade to make a stand

Madison County Historic Sites

along some ridges a few miles south of Richmond on the morning of August 30 and punish the invaders.[25]

Both armies were moving at dawn on Saturday, August 30, 1862. Cleburne's men were on the road as the day opened bright and clear. The Federals took position astride the Old State Road a mile south of the crossroads hamlet of Rogersville. Manson set his main line of battle just south of Mount Zion Church, while Union skirmishers from the 69th and 55th Indiana Regiments occupied the Kavanaugh Armstrong Farm. They did not have to wait long for action.[26]

The Federal troops had barely gotten into position when Cleburne's vanguard came into view. Despite the fact that his men were all veterans, Cleburne's division (two brigades under Brigadier General Preston Smith and Colonel Benjamin Hill) were slightly outnumbered by their rookie opponents. Cleburne set up his artillery to bombard the Federal positions and deployed Hill's brigade east of the road to tangle with the 55th Indiana. By 7:00 a.m., the Battle of Richmond was joined.[27]

As both sides groped for position, Kirby Smith rode onto the field. Intense skirmish and artillery fire signaled that the battle was well underway. Cleburne appeared to be shifting east to flank the Federals in that direction. After

Patrick Cleburne, whose division opened the battle for the Confederates. *Madison County Historic Sites*.

taking in the situation, the general determined that "my force was almost too small to storm the position in front without a disastrous loss." Kirby Smith then ordered Cleburne to (as that general reported later) "avoid a general battle until General Churchill's division could get up." The Irishman deployed Preston Smith's Tennesseans in support of Hill, and commanded his eight cannon to slow down their fire "and not waste a round."[28]

Over on the Federal side, Manson had grown very concerned about the Confederate deployment. He sent the 16th Indiana eastward to extend his flank and later stripped the forces west of the road by sending seven companies of the 69th Indiana over to the east. Meanwhile, Cruft's brigade, having breakfast in Richmond, received a message to hurry south to the sound of the guns.[29]

Manson had guessed correctly: Kirby Smith had decided to attack the Federal flank. However, while Manson expected the push to come against the eastern end of his line, the Confederate main effort was sent against the Union western flank. As Churchill's two brigades under Colonels Thomas McCray and Evander McNair arrived on the field, Kirby Smith pointed

Thomas Churchill. *Madison County Historic Sites.*

them westward to find a way around the Federal line. This division was the weakest and least experienced in the Army of Kentucky and included several regiments of Texas and Arkansas cavalry that had been permanently dismounted to fight as infantry.[30]

The 3rd Division set off on its mission with McCray's brigade in the lead. After moving west about a half mile, they came to a small creek that ran northward through a draw. The ravine's eastern face was capped with cornfields, which obstructed the view of the Armstrong Farm. This natural feature pointed like a dagger at the Federal western flank and provided a good covered approach. Without hesitation, Churchill turned his men northward and sent some Arkansas Sharpshooters in front as scouts.[31]

For two hours, Cleburne kept up his duel with the Federals. As Union troops built up to the east, he was forced to shift some of his men to respond. The Irishman rode up and down his line, exposing himself to Union fire. At one point he turned to address a wounded officer being carried from the field. Suddenly a bullet smashed into his left cheek, destroying teeth and exiting out of his mouth. Cleburne later noted that the injury "in a few minutes deprived me of the powers of speech and rendered my further presence on the field worse than useless." He turned over command to Preston Smith and left the field about 10:00 a.m.[32]

As the Confederate 4th Division sorted itself out, McCray's brigade succeeded in getting to position opposite the Federal western flank, now held by a handful of men from the 69th Indiana. Cruft's Federals now began to arrive on the field, and the 95th Ohio moved to support the 69th. At a signal from Churchill, the Confederates surged forward, catching the Federals by surprise and putting them to rout. The 95th made a short stand but soon broke under concentrated Confederate infantry and artillery fire. East of the road, Preston Smith's division attacked and cracked the Federal line, forcing it back in increasing disorder. The 18th Kentucky tried to stem the retreat but failed. By 11:00 a.m., Manson reported, the "rout had become general." The Federals made a short stand at Rogersville and then retired northward a mile to more advantageous ground at Richard White's Farm.[33]

As the Federal rookies fled before them, Kirby Smith's veterans swarmed over the field. Exhausted and exhilarated by five hours of continuous marching and fighting in rising heat, the Confederate Army of Kentucky

Looking southwest into the draw from the 69th Indiana position, 2008. Churchill's division attacked from the low ground just visible on the right side of this picture. .

stopped to regroup. Kirby Smith ordered Scott's cavalry to block the roads leading north out of Richmond and then set out with his infantry to complete the destruction of the Federals.[34]

Shortly after noon, the Confederates made contact with Manson's shaken command at White's Farm. Kirby Smith probed the line with Hill's brigade, which Cruft's men roughly handled. About this time, Nelson's order arrived directing Manson not to fight at Richmond, far too late to do any good. Cruft's Federals next launched an ill-advised counterattack that was crushed by the entire Confederate force. Kirby Smith's men lunged forward, and the Union line crumbled in panic. Within an hour of starting the fight at White's Farm, Kirby Smith had again put the Union Army of Kentucky to flight.[35]

By this point, the temperature stood at about one hundred degrees, and both sides had suffered heavily for lack of water. The Confederates stopped again to regroup, while the Federals spilled northward with little organization. Suddenly, the Confederates heard cheering, which signaled that General Nelson had arrived on the field. He had heard the firing and rode toward Richmond as fast as he could.[36]

Bull Nelson found his army in shambles, in a position approximating where it had camped the night before. He waded in among the mob of soldiers and "with great exertion" rallied about 2,200 men to make a final stand. Nelson decided to pull back to a more defensible position on the outskirts of Richmond, which he reached by 3:30 p.m. His center rested in the Richmond Cemetery and astride the Old State Road. "I was confident I could hold them in check until night, and then resume the retreat," Nelson later explained of his strategy at this point.[37]

Kirby Smith moved his men forward with deliberation. Knowing that Scott's cavalry had blocked the roads north of Richmond, he decided to make one more resolute push. Arriving before Nelson's last line about 4:00 p.m., he quickly deployed and sent his whole force forward at once. The Federals fired a few volleys and the Confederates blasted into them at short range. "Our troops stood about three volleys," recalled the Bull, and then began to waver and break. General Nelson flew into a rage and exhorted his men to stand firm, using all the language at the command of his sailor's tongue. Verbal efforts having failed, Nelson tried to stem the rout by force, hitting soldiers with his saber and reportedly shooting several of his own men until he was wounded in the thigh and taken from the field.[38]

By 5:30 p.m. it was all over, and the Federal Army of Kentucky recoiled from its third defeat of the day. The survivors fled northward in despair. Most men, including General Manson, went straight through town and tried to escape north via the Lexington Pike, where they fell into Scott's hands as prisoners. Others, including Cruft and Nelson, got out by following roads to the northeast and east. Nightfall only added to the confusion, but the conclusion was obvious: in one day, Kirby Smith had destroyed the only significant Federal force in the central Bluegrass.[39]

The Battle of Richmond ranks as arguably the most complete Confederate victory of the Civil War. Nelson's army lost 4,300 prisoners plus 1,050 killed and wounded out of 7,000 men. Kirby Smith also engaged about 7,000 men, but lost a mere 624 to all causes. Considering that this battle occurred on the same day that General Robert E. Lee drove a large Federal army at Manassas off the field in rout, August 30, 1862, has to rank as one of the best days of the Confederacy's history.[40]

The Madison County Courthouse in downtown Richmond, Kentucky. Most of the 4,300 Union prisoners were kept here after the Battle of Richmond. *Madison County Historic Sites.*

Kirby Smith paused on August 31 to replenish supplies and parole prisoners and then started for Lexington. The Army of Kentucky entered the city on September 2 to a thunderous reception. One of the Confederates remembered that "the balconies, house tops, and windows in fact every place available for view was filled with people cheering and waving handkerchiefs while we marched through the streets." Not resting on his laurels, Kirby Smith sent Scott's cavalry west toward Louisville. Other detachments from Heth's 2nd Division probed north toward Cincinnati. Frankfort fell on September 4, becoming the only capital of a loyal state captured by the Confederacy during the war.[41]

On September 6, Kirby Smith wrote to President Davis to summarize his campaign so far. He especially noted "the enthusiasm of the people here on the entry of our troops. They evidently regarded us as their deliverers from oppression and have continued in every way to prove to us that the heart of Kentucky is with the South in this struggle." Amid all the approbation, Kirby Smith did discern a threat to his gains from the Army of the Ohio: "If Bragg occupies Buell we can have nothing to oppose us [in Kentucky] but raw levies, and by the blessing of God will always dispose of them as we did on the memorable August 30."[42]

As Kirby Smith wrote those words, General Bragg's army was on the march toward Kentucky to carry out its part of the plan.

CHAPTER 3

MISSED OPPORTUNITY AT MUNFORDVILLE

When Kirby Smith moved into Kentucky in the middle of August, Bragg could not follow immediately. Rail problems had delayed the full concentration and provisioning of his troops, and the Army of the Mississippi was not ready to move northward until late August.

While waiting in Chattanooga, Bragg took the opportunity to reorganize his thirty thousand men for the coming campaign. He first wrote to President Davis denouncing most of his officers for incompetence and unsuccessfully requested sweeping powers to arrange his subordinate commanders as he saw fit. General Bragg also made it clear to everyone that he mistrusted most of his senior subordinates and their abilities. These attitudes did little but poison the command climate of the Army of the Mississippi.

Bragg created two corps-sized wing commands, each composed of two divisions. His Right Wing went to Major General Leonidas Polk, the same man whose move to Columbus a year earlier had done so much to unsettle the Western Theater. Polk was a West Point graduate but had immediately resigned from the army and had spent the last thirty-five years as an Episcopal bishop in Louisiana. He was closely connected to Confederate president Jefferson Davis and owed his high rank to Davis's patronage more than any demonstrated ability. By date of rank, the bishop was the senior wing commander in the army. The Right Wing contained two divisions led by two major generals: the competent Alabamian Jones Withers and Benjamin F. Cheatham, a hard-drinking and profane former militiaman from Nashville.[43]

Bragg's Left Wing was led by highly capable Major General William Hardee of Georgia. Hardee was one of the best-known generals on either side because he had authored a tactics manual adopted by both the Union and Confederate armies. He was a former commandant of cadets at West Point, and many high-ranking officers on both sides knew and respected his military mind. The Left Wing contained two veteran divisions commanded by Major Generals Samuel Jones of Virginia and Kentucky-born Simon Bolivar Buckner, who had just been exchanged after surrendering Fort Donelson the previous February. Jones fell ill shortly before the campaign opened and was left behind in Chattanooga; his place was taken by Brigadier General J. Patton Anderson, a Bragg loyalist from Florida.[44]

General Bragg made two other changes to the army that would prove to be significant later. First, the army's six thousand cavalrymen were divided into two equal-sized brigades under Colonels John C. Wharton and Joseph Wheeler. The two colonels reported to the wing commanders, thus ensuring that Bragg controlled no central mounted reserve to use at his discretion for scouting or screening. In Chattanooga, the army's chief of staff left his post due to sickness, and Bragg decided to wear both hats for the upcoming campaign. This dual duty meant that in addition to the strain of exercising command, devising strategy and deciding policy as army commander, he would simultaneously be immersed in the exacting administrative minutiae of a major army on campaign. This was a heavy load for any commander to bear, especially one embarking on his first operation in army command.[45]

While Bragg reorganized in Chattanooga, the Federal Army of the Ohio continued to struggle toward that city. It had not been a very pleasant summer for this army or its commander, Major General Don Carlos Buell. The Ohio-born Buell was a West Point graduate and a veteran of the Mexican War. After holding command in the Army of the Potomac for a short time, he had come west in the fall of 1861 and taken command of the Army of the Ohio. Buell was a taciturn man who tried (not always successfully) to enforce tight Regular Army discipline on the volunteer regiments in his command. Generally, his soldiers viewed him as a martinet. Like his patron George B. McClellan, Buell saw war in terms of armies moving in a vacuum with little interference from politicians or effect on the civilians in their area of operations. This conservative view especially extended to the question of slavery, and was enhanced by his family's ties to the South and slave-owning society. These attributes meant that General Buell faced nagging and unfair doubts about his loyalty to the United States.[46]

Missed Opportunity at Munfordville

After leaving Corinth in June, the Army of the Ohio moved eastward across northern Mississippi and Alabama toward Chattanooga. Low water in the Tennessee River prevented supply by the U.S. Navy, forcing Buell's army of fifty thousand men to depend on the railroads running south and southeast from Nashville for sustenance. Confederate cavalry raids and guerrillas cut the rail lines and harried the army on its advance every step of the way. Southern bandits even murdered a general, Brigadier General Robert McCook, in July. The Army of the Ohio spent much of this edgy summer on half rations.

In the face of his men's hardship, Buell forbade foraging. This order provoked much resentment in the army, and the men resorted to plundering anyway. The drought had taken its toll on local farms, and many forage parties often failed to find more provisions. This rising frustration among the Federal soldiers led to reprisals upon Confederate sympathizers, which in turn brought sharp rebukes from Buell's headquarters.[47]

At the end of August, Buell's army remained strung out on the roads and railroads leading toward Chattanooga. Two divisions under Major Generals

Buell's men on the march in Tennessee, summer 1862. *Perryville Battlefield State Historic Site.*

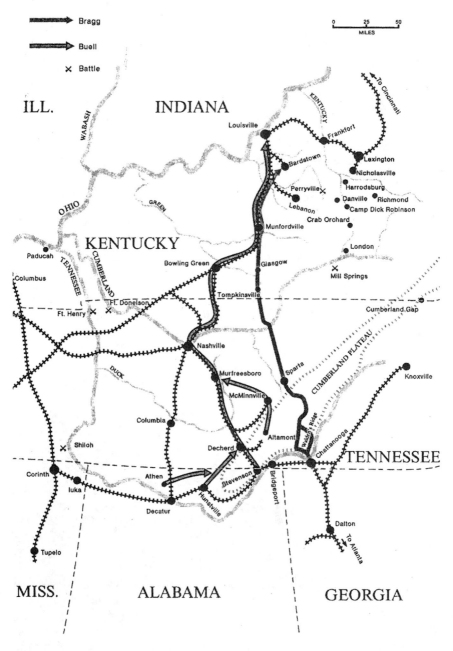

Bragg and Buell's routes to Munfordville. *Courtesy John P. Walsh Jr.*

Missed Opportunity at Munfordville

Alexander McCook and Thomas L. Crittenden stood twelve miles southwest of Chattanooga at Stevenson, Alabama. Several other components of the army stretched westward along the railroad toward Athens, Alabama. Still a third part of the army ranged between Murfreesboro and the Cumberland Plateau in a vain attempt to halt Confederate cavalry raids. This last area was a running sore of casualties for Buell as Confederate horsemen captured numerous detachments, including a major part of the Army of the Ohio's cavalry. By August 19, word of Kirby Smith's movement and Bragg's aggressive intentions caused Buell to begin concentrating near Decherd, Tennessee, to await developments.[48]

The Army of the Mississippi moved out of Chattanooga on August 28, two days before Kirby Smith's victory at Richmond. Bragg's columns wound northward over the Cumberland Plateau and arrived at Sparta, Tennessee, on September 6. Buell reacted slowly to this movement, initially favoring to fight near Sparta but instead ordering his army back to Nashville. By September 6, much of the Army of the Ohio was in that city or nearby. Reinforcements from Grant's army brought Buell's strength to approximately fifty-five thousand men.[49]

Bragg next turned north toward Kentucky. The Army of the Mississippi entered the Bluegrass State near Tompkinsville and reached the Glasgow area by September 13. The Confederates were now threatening the Louisville-Nashville Turnpike and the Louisville & Nashville (L&N) Railroad, which collectively served as Buell's lifeline between his main supply center at Louisville and the forward Federal base at Nashville. Withers's division camped that evening at Cave City, positioned to cut the turnpike and railroad. Also that night, Bragg's men made contact with John Scott's horsemen from Kirby Smith's army, who reported on the Army of Kentucky's situation around Lexington.[50]

Twelve miles north of Cave City, the turnpike and railroad crossed the Green River at Munfordville. Since the previous December, this strategic rail and road crossing, one of the most important links in Buell's supply chain, had been protected by a Federal garrison. Union troops had fortified the south side of the river with two redoubts and connecting trenches. This earthwork complex was known as Fort Craig, and it was defended by approximately two thousand infantry and artillery under Colonel John T. Wilder of Indiana. Scouts had reported Bragg's approach, and the Federal

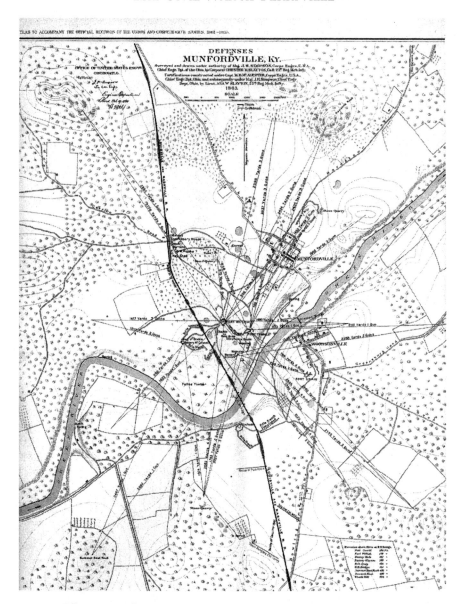

The Munfordville defenses in 1863. Note Fort Craig to the right of center. Lewis Hill is the unmarked promontory in the southeast corner. Official Atlas of the Civil War.

A sketch of the Munfordville defenses in the 1880s. *Battles and Leaders of the Civil War,* Volume III.

command in Louisville had started troops to Wilder's aid in response to his requests for help.[51]

Scott's cavalry had brushed against the Munfordville garrison on their way to meet Bragg's army. The evening of September 13, Scott demanded the fort's surrender, which Wilder promptly refused. Upon reaching Withers's lead brigade under Brigadier General James Chalmers, Scott reported to the general "that [the Federals] had from 1,200 to 1,800 men, that no re-enforcements could possibly reach them, and...their works were nothing more than rifle pits, and they perhaps unfinished, which could be easily taken by a bold dash with an infantry force." Chalmers later admitted that Scott's "information...deceived me completely."[52]

On his own, Chalmers decided to try to take Munfordville. At 10:00 p.m. on September 13, his 2,500 Mississippians took to the road again and drew up in front of Fort Craig before dawn on Sunday, September 14, 1862. Placing his four cannon atop Lewis's Hill, an eminence overlooking Fort Craig, Chalmers sent the battalion-sized Richards's Sharpshooters forward to engage the Federal pickets. He then deployed the 10th Mississippi to the west toward the Union flank, while three other regiments (7th, 9th and 29th Mississippi) attacked from the east in a coordinated pincer assault. Chalmers's last regiment, Blythe's (44th) Mississippi, remained in reserve.[53]

The first shots of the Battle of Munfordville opened at 5:00 a.m. as Richards's men made contact with Wilder's pickets. Almost immediately, Chalmers's plan broke down. On Wilder's orders, the Federal pickets quickly retreated under cover of Fort Craig before the 7th, 9th and 29th Mississippi could get in position. The Confederate artillery did not have enough range to hit Fort Craig from Lewis's Hill, and the guns were forced to move forward into Union artillery range to be effective.[54]

Suddenly, a sheet of flame engulfed the battlefield as Federal pickets set fire to some outbuildings near the fort to prevent their use by the enemy. Thinking this conflagration represented the offensive's start, Colonel R.A. Smith of the 10th Mississippi sent his men forward from the west. The Federals concentrated their fire on this regiment, killing Colonel Smith and pinning the 10th for three hours in front of the fort. Blythe's Regiment went to help and was "saluted with heavy and successive volleys of musketry," according to the unit's major. This regiment also lost its colonel and became trapped with the 10th.[55]

Over on the east side of the fort, Chalmers realized that something had gone wrong. The battle had started before all of his units got into position. Desperately, he sent the 9th and 29th into an attack; Federal artillery broke up the 9th and forced the 29th back in the face of heavy Union fire. The 7th came up to support the 29th, and both regiments attacked the works in a headlong charge. As they reached the Union parapets, artillery fire came in from their right, breaking their momentum and causing them to fall back. After parts of the 7th and Richards's Sharpshooters went to investigate, they discovered the cannon fire originated with Scott's horse artillery trying to assist. By the time the confusion was straightened out, all momentum had been lost.[56]

By 9:30 a.m. it was all over, and the Confederates pulled back to lick their wounds. Chalmers's brigade had been badly bloodied, losing 285 men killed, wounded and missing in a little over four hours. One third of the 10th Mississippi lay dead or wounded in front of Fort Craig. Wilder's losses totaled 37 men.[57]

His pride stung, Chalmers next demanded the fort's unconditional surrender. Wilder responded, "I shall defend myself until overpowered." The commanders did work out a truce, and the rest of the day was spent collecting the Confederate dead. That evening, Chalmers withdrew southward and left the Federals in peace.[58]

Missed Opportunity at Munfordville

While the fighting raged that morning, Colonel Cyrus Dunham arrived with four hundred men of the 50th Indiana. As senior officer, Dunham took command of Fort Craig after the battle. The railroad was still open to a few miles north of Munfordville, and the post had telegraph communication with the rest of the state. The Federals expected a Confederate return and spent September 15 and 16 improving the works and preparing a defense. Reinforcements streamed in, and by the morning of September 16 Munfordville had four thousand men in its garrison.[59]

At Bragg's headquarters in Glasgow, the news of Chalmers's misadventures had caused some consternation. The defeat at Munfordville represented the Army of the Mississippi's first battle under Bragg's command. General Bragg did not wish to "allow the impression of a disaster to rest on the minds of my men," and decided to reverse the debacle. Munfordville happened to be General Buckner's hometown, and his local knowledge was put to use for planning. Late on September 15, the Army of the Mississippi set out for Fort Craig.

The next morning, the Confederates made contact with Dunham's outposts and the Federals fell back into the fort. Hardee's men skirmished with the Federals while Polk's wing got into position on the Green River's north bank, where the heights dominated the Union defenses. By late afternoon on September 16, Bragg's twenty-five-thousand-man army had the Federal garrison surrounded. Confederate artillery stood ready to pound Fort Craig from all sides.[60]

Aware that he had an overwhelming advantage, Bragg sent a note to Dunham requesting surrender. The Federal reply was succinct: "Your note of this date is received. As much as I shall regret the terrible consequences of an assault upon the works under my command I shall defend them to the utmost, and God help the right." John Wilder, who delivered this message, prevailed upon Dunham to hold a council of war and consider the decision more fully. Permission from the Confederates was granted for a truce until 9:00 p.m. that evening.[61]

The telegraph line to Louisville remained open, and at 7:00 p.m., Dunham wrote to his superior, Acting Major General Charles C. Gilbert. After explaining the situation, Dunham gave vent to his doubts about the garrison's ability to hold out. Shocked by what he read, Gilbert immediately relieved Dunham and restored Wilder to command. But instead of meekly submitting

Charles Gilbert. *Perryville Battlefield State Historic Site.*

to this order, Fort Craig's senior officer wrote back to the effect that "I had so relinquished the command, and that I should take my musket and go into the trenches; that, as a senior officer, under the circumstances, I would not, as an officer, fight under a junior." Gilbert replied that Dunham should place himself under arrest and reaffirmed that Wilder once again was in charge.[62]

While this farce played out, the other senior officers of Fort Craig discussed what should be done. All of these men were in uncharted territory, since the last surrender of a sizeable United States force had occurred in 1780. (News of the previous day's capitulation at Harpers Ferry, Virginia, had not yet reached Munfordville.) In the end, Wilder explained later, "It was the unanimous expression that unless enabled by reinforcements to hold the north side of the river we could make no successful resistance. All, however, decided to resist unless full evidence should be given of the overwhelming force of the enemy." Shortly before 9:00 p.m., this request for information was sent to General Bragg.[63]

Missed Opportunity at Munfordville

The unusual Federal demand nonplussed the Confederate commander. While Bragg considered his reply, one man in the Confederate army took pity on Wilder and his predicament—Munfordville-born Simon B. Buckner. He had surrendered Fort Donelson to Grant's army the previous February and was the only senior officer on the battlefield that had experience with a capitulation. Buckner sympathized with Wilder, since he had gone through the same quandaries and agonies exactly seven months before. He intervened with Bragg, who sent back a peremptory demand for an unconditional surrender with a cover note from Buckner that read: "I am directed by General Bragg to say that no other conditions than those prescribed in his late note can be given. He requires an unconditional surrender of your forces and stores, &c., and authorizes me to accept the surrender."[64]

By this point, darkness had fallen on the field, and both armies bedded down fully expecting a major battle in the morning. About 2:00 a.m. on September 17, a blindfolded figure was led into General Buckner's tent.

Simon Bolivar Buckner.
Perryville Battlefield State Historic Site.

The visitor wore the uniform and rank of a colonel in the U.S. Army. This officer was John Wilder, who explained, "I come to you to find out what I ought to do." Buckner was staggered and a bit touched. "I wouldn't have deceived that man under those circumstances for anything," he would later explain.[65]

After giving Wilder a brief tour of Confederate positions, Buckner shared his experience as best he could with the thirty-two-year-old Indianan. "You are in command of your troops," he began, "and you must decide for yourself what you ought to do." He pointed out the ring of Confederate artillery set to open fire at daylight, and told Wilder to "judge how long your command would live under that fire." After a silence, Wilder stated that it was time to surrender. Instead of accepting the offer, Buckner replied, "No, Colonel…if you have information that would induce you to think that the sacrificing of every man at this place would gain your army an advantage elsewhere, it is your duty to do it." Wilder thought it over and concluded, "I believe I will surrender." Both men went to Bragg's tent, and in the early morning hours of September 17, 1862, John Wilder handed over the four thousand men in Fort Craig.[66]

The capitulation at Munfordville was one of the largest surrenders of U.S. troops in the Civil War. At 6:00 a.m. on September 17, the Federal garrison marched out and stacked weapons. The prisoners were paroled and sent toward Union lines. As Wilder's men vacated the post, several hundred miles to the east the Army of the Potomac and Army of Northern Virginia fought the Battle of Antietam, which resulted in nearly twenty-four thousand casualties. September 17, 1862, is the bloodiest single day in American history, with approximately twenty-eight thousand men killed, wounded, missing or captured in that twenty-four-hour period.[67]

Braxton Bragg had his first victory as an army commander. That evening he sent a dispatch to the Confederate War Department that read in part:

> *An unconditional surrender of the whole garrison was made without our firing a gun. We received some 4,000 prisoners, an equal number of small-arms, 10 pieces of artillery, and munitions. The prisoners will be paroled…My position must be exceedingly embarrassing to Buell and his army. They dare not attack me, and yet no other escape seems to be open to them.*

Missed Opportunity at Munfordville

My admiration of and love for my army cannot be expressed. To its patient toil and admirable discipline am I indebted for all the success which has attended this perilous undertaking. The men are much jaded and somewhat destitute, but cheerful and confident without a murmur.

Although this report was a bit hyperbolic, the fact remained that Bragg's army had won a great victory. With the surrender of Munfordville, Bragg's force stood between Buell's army and Louisville, in a strong position to block any northward advance by the Army of the Ohio. Coupled with Kirby Smith's success at Richmond, the Confederacy's Kentucky expedition was off to a good start.[68]

Bragg could not rest on his laurels, for General Buell had not been idle. The Army of the Ohio had left Nashville and consolidated around Bowling Green, forty miles south of Munfordville, on September 14. Buell made no effort to relieve Wilder's troops, instead preferring to draw Bragg into attacking him. Bragg, in turn, deployed for defense, expecting Buell to try and fight his way north.[69]

Shortly after Wilder's surrender, the Army of the Ohio began probing toward Munfordville. Buell moved cautiously, aware that the Green River presented a formidable defensive barrier. He also believed that Bragg's army contained about forty thousand men but lacked the cavalry to verify that estimate. The Army of the Ohio was depleting its rations, but Buell reasoned that his enemy was probably shorter on foodstuffs and might be forced into a movement to find supplies. It was this last calculation that ultimately decided the situation.[70]

Bragg's army stood in a fantastic tactical situation, but logistically it was in serious trouble. Both men and animals suffered for want of water in the worsening drought. The Federal garrison at Munfordville, in place since the previous December, had picked the local area clean of forage. The Army of the Mississippi's quartermasters reported to General Bragg that if they stayed in Munfordville more than a few days the army would begin to starve. Judging himself too weak to attack Buell, and without supplies to stay in place, Bragg was forced to make a move. Accordingly, on September 20, Bragg abandoned Munfordville and turned northeast toward Bardstown, where he expected to resupply and unite with Kirby Smith's army. Buell's road to Louisville was open. The Army of the Ohio hustled northward toward Kentucky's largest city, reaching it on September 25.[71]

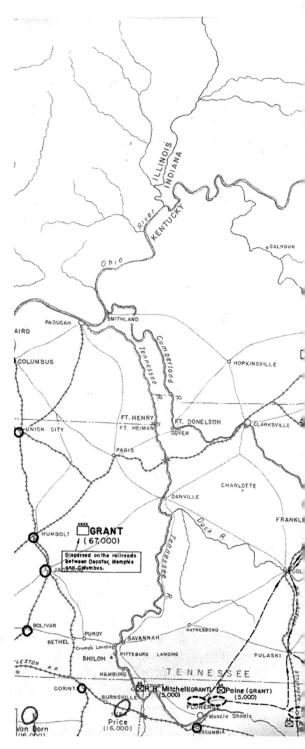

The Confederate invasion of
Kentucky to September 17, 1862.
Kirby Smith entered Lexington
on September 2 and Frankfort on
September 4. West Point Atlas of
American Wars, *author's collection*.

Missed Opportunity at Munfordville

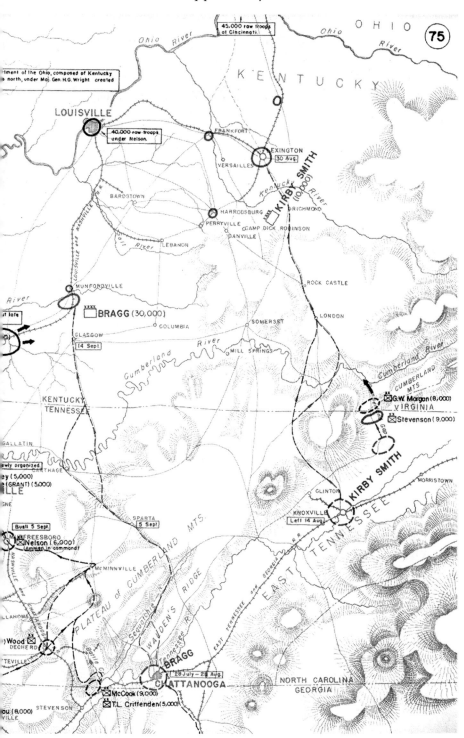

Bragg and Kirby Smith would not meet in Bardstown. While Bragg's attention was tied up at Munfordville, his counterpart focused on holding his gains in Central Kentucky. The Floridian also had a new worry: George Morgan's garrison at Cumberland Gap had suddenly become active.

CHAPTER 4

CUMBERLAND GAP

While Bragg and Buell maneuvered northward, Kirby Smith's army had spread out and secured Central Kentucky. Elements of his army pushed north and west to within ten miles of both Louisville and Cincinnati. Their arrival in Kentucky and the victory at Richmond had inflamed the North and caused considerable consternation in the states north of the Ohio River.

Henry Heth's division arrived in the southern suburbs of Cincinnati during the first week of September and stayed until September 18. Heth was content to probe the defenses with his six thousand men but did not risk an assault. Nonetheless, his arrival sparked a panic in the city and southern Ohio. Ohio governor David Tod called out citizen volunteers and sent several newly recruited regiments to the city. Local citizens (including a sizeable number of free blacks) dug trenches around Cincinnati and across the river at Covington, Kentucky.[72]

Downstream in Louisville the Federal situation was equally confused. Scott's cavalry probed the city's eastern edge on September 5, and the effect was electric. The remnants of Nelson's command from Richmond had staggered in and quickly set about digging trenches and putting the city in defensible condition. Nelson himself was in Louisville but unable to command because of his wound. General Boyle, the military governor, was making noises about instituting martial law, a move that would only inflame the situation. Casting about for a suitable commander, General Wright elevated an experienced Regular Army quartermaster, Charles Champion Gilbert, to the rank of acting major general and put him in command of

Louisville's defense. Soon the new general had restored some order to the city. Rookie regiments from the Midwest poured in, and by the middle of September over twenty thousand soldiers were on hand.[73]

While Louisville and Cincinnati buzzed with activity, the situation at Cumberland Gap represented the tense quiet of a siege. Since being isolated on August 20, George Morgan had been content with foraging and making localized probes. Cut off from the telegraph, messages had to be sent via courier over mountain roads to Cincinnati or Louisville. Carter Stevenson's nine thousand Confederates invested the post from the south, but roads to the northwest and northeast could be accessed through the thin northern Confederate cordon. Stevenson was wary of the gap's defenses and posted his pickets at a respectable distance. He was content to wait out the siege.[74]

George Morgan's Federal garrison at Cumberland Gap was known as the 7th Division of the Department of the Ohio, numbering seven thousand men. The division was split into four even-strength brigades under Colonel John F. De Courcy and Brigadier Generals Absalom Baird, James G. Spears

Carter Stevenson. *Courtesy M.C. Edwards.*

Cumberland Gap

George W. Morgan. Battles
and Leaders of the Civil War,
Volume III.

and Samuel P. Carter. Baird and De Courcy came from the North, while
Carter and Spears were both from Tennessee. A sizeable number of the men
in the 7th Division came from pro-Union East Tennessee and had relatives in
the Confederate army.[75]

Cumberland Gap itself was defended by a series of forts that capped the
promontories overlooking the Wilderness Road and the pass. Depending
on where one was stationed, part of the garrison was in Virginia, part in
Tennessee and part in Kentucky. The Confederates fortified the gap initially,
but the Federals improved the defenses after capturing it in June 1862.
Heavy cannon had been brought there, and its fortifications were so strong
as to invite comparisons with the British bastion at Gibraltar. A siege was an
engineer's battle, and Morgan had one of the best in Lieutenant William
P. Craighill, a West Point graduate, former West Point professor and future
chief engineer of the U.S. Army. Craighill had published a highly regarded
field officers' manual earlier that year. He would play an important role in
the coming days.[76]

George Morgan was initially confident that his garrison could withstand a
long siege, expecting to hold out at least five weeks. Before the telegraph was
cut, he had indicated as much to his superiors in Cincinnati and Washington.

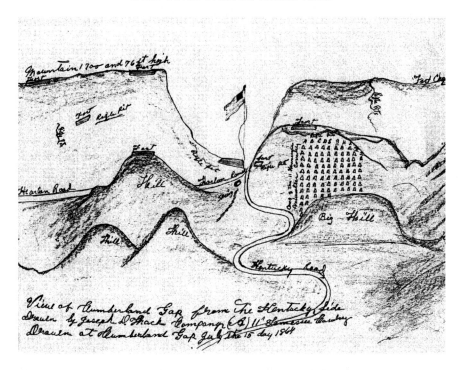

This wartime sketch shows Cumberland Gap from the north side. The prominent notch is the location of the south road closed by Lieutenant Craighill the night of the evacuation. *Courtesy M.C. Edwards.*

On August 19, the day before Kirby Smith's army blocked the Wilderness Road, 150 wagons arrived at the gap laden with provisions. Despite this boost of supplies, the Federal garrison went on half rations.[77]

Both sides stayed warily active as August turned into September. News of the Richmond debacle reached the gap a few days after the battle. In the 7th Division's camps, Confederate campfires were clearly visible in the heights to the south and west. Stevenson's pickets often skirmished with the Federal outposts, but the Confederates made no major attacks. The Union troops worked to improve their positions, while foraging parties unsuccessfully hunted for supplies in the mountains north and northeast of the gap.[78]

Preferring to avoid a passive defense, George Morgan periodically sent his men out on raids to gather information and disrupt Confederate communications. Information from prisoners and captured papers gave the Federals a fair understanding of what force opposed them. No intelligence

Cumberland Gap

This sketch of Cumberland Gap from the south appeared in *Harper's Weekly* on July 5, 1862. It approximates the view from Stevenson's Confederate positions during the siege. *Courtesy M.C. Edwards.*

arrived with regard to Federal units or movements, though. In early September, a captured dispatch brought some disconcerting news: John Hunt Morgan's cavalry was beginning to operate in the Eastern Kentucky mountains, while a small army estimated at eight to fifteen thousand men under Brigadier General Humphrey Marshall had moved into Kentucky from Southwest Virginia and was advancing northwest. The Southern grip on the gap appeared to be tightening.[79]

Meanwhile, the Federal supplies began to run out. The post's bread supply was exhausted on September 6, and other necessities soon ran dangerously low. The animals suffered just as much as the men: the 9th Ohio Battery lost most of its mules to starvation. De Courcy's brigade was sent sixty miles north to Manchester in a fruitless attempt to obtain supplies, information or reinforcements. On September 9, George Morgan sent an aide north to Cincinnati with a message in his horse collar, plus the verbal message from the general that "by eating the mules we could hold out sixty days." Three days later, the post quartermaster reported that feed for the horses and mules was almost exhausted. If these animals starved to death, the 7th Division would lose its mobility and would never be able to leave the gap.[80]

George Morgan now faced a critical decision. At 11:00 a.m. On September 14, he met with Lieutenant Craighill and Generals Baird, Spears and Carter. After considering the situation carefully, all present agreed with Craighill's statement "that in view of all the circumstances of the case the position should be evacuated."[81]

Having thus decided to leave Cumberland Gap, the next question was where to go. A march on the Old Wilderness Road toward Lexington or Central Kentucky would mean a likely encounter with Kirby Smith's entire army. In view of the 7th Division's weakened condition and lack of a supply base, a battle in the open was something to be avoided at all costs. Win or lose, George Morgan's force might be so crippled by a major fight that it would be unable to get to Union lines.

The only other alternative was to go through the mountains to the Ohio River, two hundred miles to the north. This route led away from Kirby Smith's main strength, which was its chief advantage. But this option also meant a major movement into a wild region using narrow roads and defiles that could easily be blocked by an intrepid opponent. George Morgan had marked a possible route on a map, and he showed it to some officers who were familiar with Eastern Kentucky's mountains. Almost to a man they agreed that it would be a tough road, with little forage or water to be found. One officer, the former Kentucky state geologist, said that the 7th Division could "possibly" get through, but only "by abandoning the artillery and wagons." Despite the risks, the 7th Division's commander decided to try to bring his whole force out through the mountains.[82]

On September 16, orders went out to prepare for a movement on the evening of September 17. Anything that could not be taken along was to be destroyed. Lieutenant Craighill was given a special mission: blowing up the pass through the gap itself and blocking the road from the south so as to delay Stevenson's pursuit. That evening, the first wagon train moved toward Manchester.[83]

On September 17, the Cumberland Gap garrison performed the delicate task of preparing for evacuation while trying to keep the Confederates unaware of what was happening. Men packed wagons and their personal belongings, while others prepared the post buildings for demolition. Four large cannon that could not be taken along were spiked and thrown over a cliff. At

Cumberland Gap

A wartime postcard photograph of the gap from the north side. This image gives an idea of the buildings and infrastructure that made up the post at Cumberland Gap. *Courtesy M.C. Edwards.*

headquarters, the route was finalized; the division would leave at 8:00 p.m., pause at Manchester and move north by northeast to Greenupsburg (present-day Greenup) on the Ohio River.[84]

Late in the afternoon, a group of Confederates was seen approaching the Federal picket line. Fearful that the evacuation had been given away, George Morgan sent the post provost marshal, Lieutenant Colonel George W. Gallup, and a party to meet them under a flag of truce. The two delegations conferred between the lines, and it soon developed that the Confederates were on a scouting mission. Gallup engaged them in conversation when suddenly flames blazed up from the gap. Someone had prematurely set fire to one of the warehouses in the valley.[85]

It was a bad moment for the whole garrison. Suspicious, one of the Confederates asked Gallup, "Why Colonel, what does that mean? It looks like an evacuation." Without skipping a beat, Gallup replied, "Not much. Morgan has cut away the timber obstructing the range of his guns, and they are now burning the brush on the mountainside." This explanation seemed to suffice, and shortly thereafter both parties returned to their lines.[86]

As darkness fell, the 7th Division made its final preparations to leave. At 8:00 p.m., the garrison formed up in the gap and set off toward Manchester. Spears's East Tennessee regiments were the last to leave, some embittered at having to turn their backs on their homes. By 10:00 p.m., the post was almost deserted save for two hundred picked men commanded by Colonel Gallup. His detachment set fire to the various buildings in the gap; one participant later noted that soon "the little valley, encircled by the mountains at the foot of the Gap, was one sea of flame."[87]

At this point the Confederates became very suspicious and probed the Union position. Gallup's pickets held them at bay. After midnight, the area rocked with explosions as the engineers blew up the forts and the powder magazine. Craighill's charges successfully blocked the south road into the gap. These explosions could be seen several miles away; an observer later described how "the flaming buildings lighted up the sky as though the Gap and mountain crests were a volcano on fire, and from time to time till after dawn we heard the explosion of mines, shells, or grenades." As dawn approached, Gallup's detachment marched out amid what George Morgan later reported was "the explosion of mines and magazines and lighted by the blaze of the store-houses of the commissary and quartermaster." After more than four weeks of siege, the 7th Division had evacuated Cumberland Gap.[88]

By September 19, the entire garrison and its five hundred wagons had arrived at Manchester. Stevenson's infantry was delayed at the gap, but Confederate cavalry nipped at the wagon train. The 7th Division could not stay idle, so George Morgan turned to the next part of the movement. North of the town, the road forked. One road led northwest toward Richmond and Lexington, while the other ran north toward the hamlet of Proctor (present-day Beattyville) on the Kentucky River. John Hunt Morgan's cavalry was known to be active in that area. George Morgan had to get to the bridge at Proctor before his namesake opponent destroyed it. After pausing a day to reorganize, the 7th Division moved north. Its columns snaked several miles long through the mountains.[89]

In Lexington, September 19 brought Kirby Smith news of George Morgan's abandonment of Cumberland Gap. Also on that day came notice of Bragg's success at Munfordville and request for assistance to move against Louisville. Based on information he had received (including a decoy from George

Cumberland Gap

Manchester, Kentucky, in the late nineteenth century. *Courtesy M.C. Edwards.*

Morgan), it appeared that the 7th Division was heading straight north from the gap to Maysville on the Ohio River. Kirby Smith was also ignorant of the Federal supply situation and expected George Morgan to seek battle. In Kirby Smith's mind, this surge from Cumberland Gap represented a serious threat.[90]

Torn between two opposing directions, Kirby Smith compromised as best he could. In a flurry of orders from Lexington, he dispatched the 4th Division (once again under a recovered Patrick Cleburne) west toward Shelbyville and Louisville. A supply convoy also moved west to meet Bragg at Bardstown. Meanwhile, Heth's 2nd Division was recalled from Cincinnati and sent east of Lexington to Mount Sterling. John Morgan was ordered to take his cavalry (including some fresh recruits) to Irvine, twenty-six miles west of Proctor. Stevenson received instructions to pursue George Morgan as best he could. Humphrey Marshall, defiantly independent of Kirby Smith's command, was requested to cooperate with Heth and John Morgan to block and surround George Morgan's division in the mountains.[91]

These orders effectively concentrated the Confederate army to the northwest of Proctor, astride the 7th Division's expected path. Instead, the Federals turned northeast and reached Proctor on September 21. They found that John Morgan's cavalry had been through there the night before on the way to Irvine. Proctor's flour mill had been burned but the bridge was intact. George Morgan was surprised at the lack of opposition, as he would later write:

> *I fully expected to be met by the enemy in force at Proctor, where the deep and abrupt banks would have rendered the passage of the Kentucky River perilous and difficult if disputed. We accordingly moved by two nearly parallel roads, and the two columns reached Proctor almost simultaneously. I at once threw a brigade, with a battery, across the river, and gave the command half a day's rest.*

Kirby Smith's order to John Morgan's cavalry had moved them twenty-six miles out of the way and denied the Confederates their first opportunity to stop the 7th Division's northward progress.[92]

After a short rest, the 7th Division resumed its northward march. The next stop was the hamlet of Hazel Green, thirty miles away. John Morgan had realized the Confederate error and moved eastward as fast as the terrain allowed. Too late to block the 7th Division's march, he was content to harass the flanks and rear of the Union column. George Morgan later reported that "the route to Hazel Green was [very] difficult. The ridge was almost entirely destitute of water, and where it did exist it was found in small quantities in holes down 80 or 100 feet among cliffs. The North Fork Road had been destroyed by the spring and winter rains, but water was plentiful." Baird's and De Courcy's brigades escorted the wagons and artillery along the North Fork Road, while Spears's and Carter's Tennesseans moved along the ridge roads above. Fighting both the relentless terrain and John Morgan's cavalry took a lot of energy from George Morgan's half-starved men, but the Federals made inexorable progress. The 7th Division reached Hazel Green on September 23 and paused one day for a much-needed rest.[93]

The next stage of the march, twelve miles from Hazel Green to West Liberty, showed a new aggressiveness from the Confederates. John Morgan's cavalry attacked the 6th Tennessee Infantry (U.S.) at the rear of the column, killing six men and scattering eighty to one hundred head of cattle before being driven off. Meanwhile, Confederate infantry closed in but failed to move fast enough to catch the Federals in the passes. Some of Humphrey Marshall's troops got close to the 7th Division but shrank from battle due to being outnumbered. George Morgan's division staggered into West Liberty on September 25 and paused two days to rest and offer battle.[94]

The forty-three miles from West Liberty to Grayson proved to be the toughest part of the march, thanks to John Morgan and his intrepid horsemen. John Morgan got around in front of the Federal column and immediately set about trying to hinder or stop the 7th Division's progress. His men used every means at their disposal, including barricading roads and laying ambushes. George Morgan had no choice but to run this gauntlet; he later described how

> *frequent skirmishes took place, and it several times happened that while the one Morgan was clearing out the obstructions at the entrance to a defile, the other Morgan was blocking the exit from the same defile with enormous rocks and felled trees. In the work of clearing away these obstructions, one thousand men, wielding axes, saws, picks, spades, and block and tackle, under the general direction of Captain William F. Patterson, commanding his company of engineer-mechanics, and of Captain Sidney S. Lyon, labored with skill and courage. In one instance they were forced to cut a new road through the forest for a distance of four miles in order to turn a blockade of one mile.*

The Confederates succeeded in slowing George Morgan's pace to a mere six miles per day. Yet the 7th Division also struck back, as George Morgan later reported: "Whenever opportunity offered we assumed the offensive and attacked the enemy while engaged in blockading the road. On three successive evenings so closely did we push him that we drove him from his hot supper."[95]

This cat-and-mouse hunt lasted for five days until the Federals reached Grayson on the evening of October 1. Earlier that day, John Morgan had been ordered to rejoin Kirby Smith, as developments elsewhere required his attention. Two days later, George Morgan's force arrived at Greenupsburg on the Ohio River, where some of his men found the water so low that many of the wagons could ford. On October 3, the 7th Division crossed into Ohio and safety.[96]

The men of George Morgan's 7th Division had made one of the epic marches in American military history. In sixteen days they covered 219 miles through some of the wildest terrain in the eastern United States, battling Confederates, topography and dwindling sustenance the entire way. George Morgan outwitted his opponents at every turn and succeeded in foiling John Morgan's persistent attempts to stop the Federal movement. Since leaving Cumberland Gap, the Federals had lost eighty men killed, wounded and missing/deserted but brought out all their baggage and artillery.[97]

While this mountain odyssey played out, two hundred miles westward a very different drama unfolded as Buell and Bragg maneuvered north of Munfordville.

CHAPTER 5

TURMOIL IN LOUISVILLE

After leaving Munfordville, Bragg's Army of the Mississippi headed northeast forty miles to Bardstown. It was a tough march, with many men reportedly going barefoot. The heat and drought added to their miseries, but the Confederates sensed that an opportunity had slipped by. Lieutenant John Inglis of the 3rd Florida spoke for many when he wrote, "We were vexed in not stopping" the Federals, and that Bragg's troops were "eager to fight them." Despite the disappointment at Munfordville, the army remained "generally cheerful, confident & happy," one of Anderson's brigade commanders noted.[98]

The army's spirits were lifted by their reception in Bardstown on September 23. The town's welcome to the Army of the Mississippi was comparable to how Lexington greeted Kirby Smith's army. Lieutenant Inglis remembered that the army paraded through town while Bragg reviewed it on the courthouse steps with Generals Buckner, Anderson, Polk and others. But the young officer's attention was not solely directed at his commanders: "The ladies look so sweet," he confided to his diary.[99]

The Army of the Mississippi set up camp around Bardstown and its various approach roads. Kirby Smith's supplies helped bring the army back to fighting trim, and Cleburne's division was absorbed back into the army. Meanwhile, some men took advantage of the locals' hospitality, while others foraged in the nearby countryside. Quite a few Confederates got acquainted with bourbon, the town's most famous product.[100]

Despite the welcome interlude, several shadows now began to loom over the Kentucky expedition. First was the decided reluctance of male

Kentuckians to join the Confederate army. Bragg had brought 15,000 rifles with him into Kentucky and expected to find plenty of demand for them. Unfortunately, the expected wave of recruits did not materialize. Camp Dick Robinson was renamed Camp Breckinridge, and General Buckner was sent there to muster recruits. Despite issuing a statewide appeal, he succeeded in raising only about 1,500 soldiers. Efforts to boost recruiting by transferring favorite sons John C. Breckinridge and the Orphan Brigade soldiers to Kentucky from Louisiana ran afoul of delays. In the end, only about 5,000 Kentuckians joined the Confederate army, and most of those went into the cavalry.[101]

This lack of enthusiasm did not go unnoticed in the Confederate ranks. Kirby Smith lamented that Kentuckians' "hearts are evidently with us, but their blue-grass and fat-grass [cattle] are against us." There was something to this theory, as the Union authorities had issued several decrees that ensured that pro-Confederates who fought placed their property at risk of confiscation. With sizeable Federal forces in and around Louisville, many in the state realized that the campaign had only just begun. Bragg and Kirby Smith needed to assure the populace that the Confederacy was there to stay.[102]

Some of Bragg's cavalrymen pose for the camera in camp. *Perryville Battlefield State Historic Site.*

Turmoil in Louisville

Bragg's mood darkened as he realized how hesitant Kentucky recruits were proving to be. People around army headquarters began to notice that the general was developing an increasing disdain for all things Kentucky. Bragg's frustration came through in a dispatch to the Confederate War Department on September 25:

> *I regret to say we are sadly disappointed at the want of action by our friends in Kentucky. We have so far received no accession to this army. General Smith has secured about a brigade—not half our losses by casualties of different kinds. We have 15,000 stand of arms and no one to use them. Unless a change occurs soon we must abandon the garden spot of Kentucky to its cupidity. The love of ease and fear of pecuniary loss are the fruitful sources of this evil. Kentucky and Tennessee are redeemed if we can be supported, but at least 50,000 men will be necessary, and a few weeks will decide the question. Should we have to retire, much in the way of supplies and* morale *will be lost, and the redemption of Kentucky will be indefinitely postponed, if not rendered impossible.*

The strain of holding two posts added to his burden, and the general showed signs of buckling under the heavy responsibilities inherent in army command. In late September, General Bragg appointed George W. Brent chief of staff for the Army of the Mississippi.[103]

Another factor that dampened Confederate ardor was the strategically bankrupt position occupied by the Army of the Mississippi. Bragg's army at Bardstown stood forty miles from Louisville and was in a good position to interdict any Federal surge from that city. However, the Confederates were too far away to menace or harass Buell. Bragg's thirty thousand men at Bardstown needed Kirby Smith's eighteen thousand at Lexington to face the Federals on something close to even terms, but the Floridian showed little sign of wishing to leave the vicinity of Lexington. Until the two generals joined forces on the field, Bragg could not assume formal command as senior officer. The Confederacy controlled virtually all of Central and Eastern Kentucky, but its forces were spread out and subject to defeat in detail. George Morgan's movement northward worried Bragg, as did the formidable defenses of Louisville and Cincinnati. The central supply and recruiting depot at Camp Breckinridge also needed protection. Too weak to attack, and thinking Buell would need weeks to refit his force in Louisville, Bragg decided to pause and consolidate. The Confederates went on the defensive in Kentucky, passing the initiative to the Union.[104]

Buell's veterans staggered into Louisville over four days, September 25–28. In the space of one month they had been forced to withdraw three hundred miles from the Tennessee River near Chattanooga back to the Ohio without fighting a major battle and almost without firing a shot. The situation stung the Federals' pride, especially on top of the frustrating summer. The vast majority of these veterans also had worn out their uniforms and equipment, and most had not been paid in months. New uniforms and some pay were available in Louisville, sometimes at the expense of the rookie regiments that comprised the city's garrison. When they hit the town, many veterans took the opportunity to blow off some steam at the local bars. Others, especially those soldiers from southern Indiana, went home for a few days without permission. The Army of the Ohio partially disintegrated for a short time but came back together by September 30 with restored spirits. Unlike their comrades in the East, Buell's soldiers had little comment about the announcement of Lincoln's preliminary Emancipation Proclamation on September 22.[105]

General Buell's stock was at a nadir, and some of his subordinates pushed openly for a command change. In Washington, the War Department had also decided that a new commander was necessary. General in Chief Halleck sent a courier westward with orders relieving Buell and replacing him with Major General George Thomas, a respected and experienced Virginian who had remained loyal to the Union. The orders were not to take effect "if General Buell should be found in the presence of the enemy preparing to fight a battle." The relief directive arrived on September 29, finding Buell's army in the midst of organizing, supplying and planning for a major campaign into Central Kentucky.[106]

When he received the dispatch, Buell immediately moved to turn over command. The problem was that Thomas refused to take it. As the Virginian wrote to Halleck, "General Buell's preparations have been completed to move against the enemy, and I therefore respectfully ask that he may be retained in command. My position is very embarrassing, not being as well informed as I should be as the commander of this army and on the assumption of such a responsibility." Exasperated but unwilling to referee, Halleck informed both men that the orders were "suspended" and confirmed that General Buell retained command. Yet Buell still had the prospect of relief hanging over him at any moment.[107]

When the relief orders arrived, Buell had been busy reorganizing the army's command structure for the upcoming campaign. The new recruits swelled his army's strength to seventy-five thousand men, but most of them needed training beyond the rudiments they had received at home. The rookies threatened to hamper the Army of the Ohio's marching and fighting power. Instead of grouping the new units together, Buell parceled most of them out among his veteran brigades, three veteran outfits for each green unit. The exceptions to this policy were the 10th Division, which was made up of all rookie units and commanders, and parts of the 11th Division.[108]

Buell managed to keep his job on September 29, but that day he did lose an experienced subordinate. Bull Nelson had recovered from his Richmond wound and was back on duty when the Army of the Ohio arrived in Louisville. His experiences at Richmond had given him a poor impression of Indiana troops, and General Nelson made no secret of his dislike of Hoosiers. This attitude bristled on Brigadier General Jefferson C. Davis, a prickly Indianan who took great pride in his state. The two men got into a shouting match, and Nelson sent him to Cincinnati under arrest on September 25. General Wright released him from arrest and ordered him back to Louisville and the Army of the Ohio. Davis returned with Indiana governor Levi Morton, who happened to be going there on an inspection trip.[109]

About 7:30 on the morning of September 29, Davis, Morton and several aides ran into Nelson in the lobby of the Galt House hotel in downtown Louisville. The two generals exchanged words, and Nelson slapped Davis. As the Bull walked away, an enraged Davis grabbed a pistol from an aide and followed Nelson upstairs. After some more words, Davis shot Nelson in the chest. The Bull collapsed and died an hour later, and Davis was placed under arrest. At a stroke, one of Buell's potential senior commanders was removed from the scene.[110]

Later that day, General Buell announced his command structure for the upcoming campaign. For the first time in its history, the Army of the Ohio would contain corps, numbered I, II and III. Each corps contained about twenty-five thousand men and brought infantry, artillery and cavalry under a single commander. Thomas, whom Buell now viewed as a threat, was elevated to the sinecure of second in command of the army.[111]

Command of I Corps went to Major General Alexander McCook of Ohio, one of Buell's most experienced subordinates. General McCook was a flamboyant character known for his appetite, fleshy figure and luxurious lifestyle. He had a good résumé, including a stint as tactics instructor at West Point. The general was one of fourteen in his family to serve in the Union army during the Civil War; his older brother Robert had been killed by Confederate raiders a few months before. McCook's corps contained Brigadier General Joshua Sill's 2nd Division, Brigadier General Lovell Rousseau's 3rd Division and Brigadier General James S. Jackson's 10th Division. All three were experienced commanders; Rousseau and Jackson were both Kentuckians, while Sill came from Ohio.[112]

Major General Thomas L. Crittenden received command of II Corps. Unlike McCook's pro-Union clan, secession had torn apart this general's family and friends. Crittenden's residence was in Louisville, and he was an old friend of Simon B. Buckner from their service in the Kentucky State Guard. His alcoholic older brother was a major general in the Confederate army and would soon resign his commission in disgrace. General Crittenden's father was the senior U.S. senator from Kentucky who in 1861 unsuccessfully tried to broker a compromise between the United States and the Confederacy. The senator had a home in Frankfort that was occupied by Confederates. Crittenden's II Corps divisions were all led by experienced brigadiers: William Sooy Smith led the 4th Division, Horatio Van Cleve directed the 5th Division and Thomas J. Wood commanded the 6th Division. Sooy Smith and Van Cleve came from the North; Wood was a Kentuckian and boyhood best friend of General Buckner.[113]

Bull Nelson was originally selected to lead III Corps, but his murder removed that possibility. Its three divisions were the 1st under Brigadier General Albin Schoepf, Brigadier General Robert B. Mitchell's 9th Division and the new 11th Division, belonging to Brigadier General Philip H. Sheridan. All three were aggressive officers and had led divisions before except Sheridan. Mitchell and Sheridan were Ohioans, while Schoepf was a Polish immigrant who had experience in the Austrian army. Schoepf was the logical choice for corps command, but he disliked Buell intensely and had openly campaigned for a new army commander. Casting about for someone he could work with, Buell settled on Acting Major General Gilbert and put him in charge of the corps.[114]

Alexander McCook. *Perryville Battlefield State Historic Site.*

Many of the Army of the Ohio's leaders were in their posts for the first time. Most of the newly promoted men settled into their new jobs with little problem, but several officers had rough starts in their commands. Jackson and one of his brigade commanders, William R. Terrill, drilled their men for hours in high temperatures and had a grand review that resulted in numerous heat-related casualties and four deaths. Gilbert enjoyed micromanaging his troops, including rifling through officers' baggage. His profanity and arrogant attitude alienated many III Corps soldiers and set a poor tone for the upcoming campaign.[115]

The next question for Buell and the army was what to do. Staying on the defensive was out of the question, so the general decided to advance. Two options presented themselves: the army could go eastward to Frankfort or southeast through Bardstown into Central Kentucky. Looking at a map, Buell saw that the Confederate supply base was at Camp Breckinridge and their only line of communication back to Tennessee was via the Wilderness Road. Moving into Central Kentucky would threaten that road and force the Confederates to withdraw and protect their lifeline. In that event, Frankfort and Lexington would be liberated easier than if the Army of the Ohio advanced on them directly.

Based on this shrewd calculation, Buell made his decision. Thomas later described the plan in simple terms: "The object was to overtake the enemy, fight, and destroy him if possible, either by a disastrous defeat or by cutting off his retreat." Buell divided his army into four columns. General Sill's 2nd Division was detached from I Corps and ordered east toward Frankfort and Lexington as a feint. A provisional command of rookie troops under Colonel Ebenezer Dumont would go along, bringing Sill's force to twenty thousand men. The other fifty-five thousand men of the Army of the Ohio would form three columns and move toward Bardstown and beyond, looking for battle. Hopefully, the Confederates would be snared by the four heads of the Federal hydra and defeated or forced back into Tennessee. It was an excellent plan that offered a good prospect of success.[116]

While Buell made his preparations, Bragg turned over command at Bardstown to General Polk and rode to Lexington. After asserting control of all Confederate forces in Kentucky, Bragg discussed options with Kirby Smith. Governor Richard Hawes and some of his provisional government legislators had followed the army into the state and were on hand. Bragg decided to install this government, hoping that by grasping the levers of civil power he could stimulate recruiting or compel a draft. Hawes proved a willing partner, and an installation ceremony was planned in Frankfort for October 4.[117]

On October 1, Buell's legions moved out from Louisville after spending less than a week in the city. What took place over the next eleven days would decide the fate of Kentucky.

CHAPTER 6

ROADS TO PERRYVILLE

On October 1, 1862, the situation for the Union in Kentucky was critical. The Confederates controlled virtually the entire state east of the Louisville & Nashville Railroad and were on the verge of installing a civil government to tighten their grip on the Bluegrass State. Buell needed to wage a victorious campaign; otherwise, Kentucky could be irretrievably lost to the Confederacy. The stakes could not have been higher for the Army of the Ohio as it left Louisville.

The Federal columns departed the city by four roads. Sill's 2nd Division marched east on the Shelbyville Turnpike, aiming for Frankfort, fifty miles distant. McCook's corps followed the Taylorsville Road, forming the left flank of Buell's main thrust to the southeast. Crittenden took the center on the Bardstown Road, while Gilbert's corps anchored the Federal right on the Shepherdsville Pike. Thomas rode with Crittenden's troops, while Buell accompanied Gilbert's column. Cavalry preceded all the infantry columns and ranged ahead for Confederates. By the first night, the Federals were ten miles outside of Louisville and well on their way.[118]

The greenhorn regiments slowed the Federal advance, most of them not yet accustomed to campaigning. A lot of the rookies were carrying too much gear and soon began to dump their loads to the side. Private Timothy Pendergast of the 2nd Minnesota described how "we began to see fine new boots lying by the roadside, alongside of new blankets, shoes, fine shirts, books, and all kinds of trinkets for use or ornament...scarcely half of the new regiments kept their place in the ranks until camp was reached. The remainder were scattered along the road for several miles, nursing blistered feet or aching backs, while of the [veteran] troops scarcely one [man] was missing." Those veterans who lacked new equipment availed themselves of this roadside bonanza along the army's line of march.[119]

Buell's advance caught the Confederates still around Bardstown. The Southern cavalry had pushed farther northward, but after weeks of uninterrupted patrolling their mounts were run-down and less effective than at the start of the campaign. Their Federal counterparts were newly organized and reequipped from Louisville and provided Buell with a fair picture of the Confederate dispositions. The Confederates detected Buell's march on October 2, and Polk reported the information to Bragg in Lexington.[120]

Polk's message found General Bragg in fine spirits, busily planning Richard Hawes's inauguration on October 4. Thinking the Frankfort advance was Buell's main effort, and lacking a cavalry force under his control to verify that estimate, Bragg decided to concentrate the Army of Kentucky and the Army of the Mississippi west of Kentucky's capital and offer battle. Bragg wished to use Kirby Smith's command as a blocking force from the east while Polk came up from the southwest and smashed into the Federals from the flank. He immediately ordered Polk to "put your whole available force in motion by Bloomfield and strike him in flank and rear. If we can combine our movements he [Buell] is certainly lost." Instead of postponing the ceremonies for Governor Hawes and taking command in the field, Bragg continued with preparations for the October 4 events. The handling of troops fell to Polk and Kirby Smith, neither of whom fully understood the situation in Kentucky or Bragg's plans. That evening, Generals Bragg, Smith and Buckner set off for Frankfort with Heth's 2nd Division, where they were to meet Stevenson's 1st Division.[121]

Bragg's orders put Polk in a dilemma. Buell's intentions had since become clearer; the Federal main effort was clearly aimed at Bardstown, not Frankfort. One Federal column was on its way directly to Bardstown, while flanking forces threatened to envelop the Army of the Mississippi from the west and east. Each passing day brought Buell's legions ten to twelve miles closer; by the morning of October 3, the Federals stood about a day's march from Bardstown. Moving as ordered would cause the Confederates to collide with McCook's thirteen-thousand-strong I Corps near Bloomfield, east of Bardstown. Fighting McCook would delay the Confederate movement to Frankfort and would enable the rest of Buell's army to concentrate and smash Polk's force. Aware that he was outnumbered almost two to one, Polk needed to make a decision quickly.

Late on the morning of October 3, the bishop called a council of war with his division and wing commanders. After reading the order from Bragg to move through Bloomfield, Polk solicited discussion. Only Patton Anderson, a Bragg loyalist, argued to follow the order. When asked what he would council if no order had existed, Anderson suggested a withdrawal eastward toward Harrodsburg, forty miles away. Everyone agreed, Polk later wrote, that "we were all clearly satisfied as to the position of the troops of the enemy, which information we were sure the general commanding the forces could not have, or he would not have issued such an order." Not wishing to risk a battle without the close support of the Army of Kentucky, Polk decided to retire eastward.[122]

While the Confederates prepared to evacuate, McCook's Federals nearby stumbled upon one of the social fault lines in Kentucky. A slave state, the commonwealth was not bound by Lincoln's recent Emancipation

J. Patton Anderson. *Perryville Battlefield State Historic Site.*

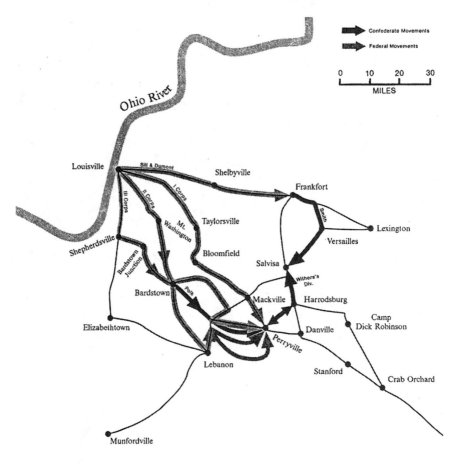

Buell's advance to Perryville in the first week of October 1862. *Courtesy John P. Walsh Jr.*

Proclamation. During a stop in Bloomfield on the evening of October 3, an escaped slave appeared in the 21st Wisconsin's camp, followed shortly by three men chasing him and demanding his return. The 21st was a new unit, having just been raised the previous August. The regiment's colonel, Benjamin Sweet, replied that he would "give no assistance in running after" the escapee. According to Lieutenant Michael Fitch, the 21st's adjutant, "the slave masters not liking the chilling northern aspect of the soldiers, [appealed to] division headquarters." The 21st belonged to Colonel John C. Starkweather's 28th Brigade of Lovell H. Rousseau's 3rd Division. General Rousseau was a slave-owning Kentuckian, and he ordered the fugitive

Lovell Rousseau. *Perryville Battlefield State Historic Site.*

turned over to his pursuers. This order should have closed the matter, but the aide delivering the message got into a dispute over the case with some 21st soldiers and was run "out of camp, with corn-cobs flying in rather close proximity about his head," according to Fitch, who noted that "this episode was not seen from the headquarters of the regiment."[123]

When General Rousseau heard how his aide had been treated, he flew into a rage. Mounting his horse, he ordered the rest of Starkweather's brigade formed in a hollow square and under arms, with the 21st unarmed in the center. An observer described what happened next:

> *Thus standing, he addressed the twenty-first saying he would kill the man or men who attacked his orderly, and was determined to find out who it was.* [Colonel Sweet] *immediately called upon any man who had thrown at the orderly to step forward from the ranks. A half-dozen or more, without the least hesitation, stepped out. They were marched off to division headquarters and the parade dismissed.*

Colonel Sweet and his staff appealed to Rousseau and explained the situation. The general backed off and released the prisoners back to the ranks. In the meantime, the slave who caused all this commotion escaped free and clear.[124]

Early on October 4, the Army of the Mississippi abandoned Bardstown. The Right Wing moved southeast via Springfield toward Danville, while Hardee's Left Wing started via Mackville toward Harrodsburg. Both wings were never more than ten miles apart and were in a good position to protect the vital base at Camp Breckinridge.[125]

As the last of the Confederates pulled out, the first elements of Crittenden's II Corps arrived on the north side of town. Wharton's cavalry fought a sharp engagement before evacuating to join the infantry as protection. Wheeler's horsemen also assumed rear guard duties as the Army of the Mississippi snaked eastward.[126]

October 4 was inauguration day in Frankfort, and Bragg rose early. After receiving word of Polk's decision and actions, Bragg ordered him

John C. Wharton. *Perryville Battlefield State Historic Site.*

to concentrate at Harrodsburg. Despite the fluid military situation and entreaties from Kirby Smith and Buckner to postpone, Bragg went ahead with the installation ceremony. "We shall put our Governor in power soon and then I propose to seek the enemy," he said.[127]

Shortly before noon, Richard Hawes arrived at the Kentucky State Capitol[128] to be installed as governor of Confederate Kentucky. A salvo of Confederate artillery announced his arrival, and he went upstairs to the House chamber. The room was too small to hold the crowd that attended the event, and the overflow spilled into the rotunda. Kentucky native Humphrey Marshall spoke, followed by a grandiose address from Bragg. Then the chief executive came to the podium. Hawes had been sworn in earlier that year, but he did read an address that pledged that his government would stay in Frankfort and that the Federal troops would soon be expelled from the state.[129]

A luncheon followed the ceremony. While the guests enjoyed their meal and looked forward to a ball that evening, artillery fire suddenly erupted to the west. The sound meant that Sill's Federals had arrived to liberate the city. Bragg ordered everyone to "skedaddle," as Kirby Smith put it, and after dismantling Frankfort's bridges over the Kentucky River, the Confederates abandoned the city. That evening, Sill's column reoccupied the capital, ending its thirty-day occupation by the Confederacy. Considering the day's rhetoric, being chased out of Frankfort was a bitter pill; one of Bragg's staff officers noted that "a paralysis of gloom settled" over the escapees as they rode away from the capital city.[130]

Buell spent October 4 regrouping in Bardstown and then set out eastward the next day. Gilbert's III Corps took the direct road through Springfield, while McCook and Crittenden marched on parallel roads to the north and south, respectively. Sill's troops also left Frankfort on October 5 and started a slow march southward to join Buell.[131]

Just one hundred hours into the Union counteroffensive, the Confederate Kentucky invasion was unraveling. The Southerners had lost Frankfort and stood to possibly lose the rest of Central Kentucky. Bragg frantically looked for a place to fight, and after considering Versailles (fifteen miles west of Lexington), he settled on Harrodsburg as the place to give battle against Buell and Sill. Harrodsburg was close to Camp Breckinridge, while the town's road network would enable him to access most of Central Kentucky.

Bragg rode south to that place and ordered both Confederate armies to join him there.[132]

Meanwhile, Buell's Federals chased Polk's Confederates eastward through the central Bluegrass. During the march, the heat and drought took their toll on the soldiers of both sides. Intermittent rain did little to alleviate the parched conditions. Most of the rivers and streams were dry or nearly so, and the effect was sharpened by the fact that thirsty Confederates usually depleted the water supplies before the Union pursuers reached them. A Minnesotan in Gilbert's corps recalled, "On the 4th we crossed Salt River, without wetting our shoes, where the winter before it had been twenty feet deep."[133]

The Federal troops by this point had started to take the measure of their new commanders. Colonel John Beatty of the 3rd Ohio in Rousseau's division described that general as "by far the handsomest man in the army" and commended his bravery. The corps commander cut a less impressive figure, however: "McCook is a chucklehead [and] has a grin, which excites the suspicion that he is either still very green or deficient in the upper story." In III Corps, Gilbert's harsh command style continued to alienate his troops, and on at least one occasion he had to be led away from his men lest they try and kill him.[134]

Sparks flew while the armies moved eastward, as cavalry of both sides clashed between the infantry columns. Hardee had been forced to shift southward and now was being pressed closely by Gilbert's corps. Wheeler's horsemen managed to keep the Federals at bay, even turning the tables on their counterparts at Pottsville on October 7. That evening, Wheeler's men drew back two miles to the vicinity of Perryville, a small crossroads hamlet where Hardee's two divisions had stopped. The Federals halted about three miles west of town. With the enemy on its heels, the Confederate Left Wing needed some help if it was to continue its withdrawal unmolested. When informed of the situation, Bragg wrote Polk to take Cheatham's division of the Right Wing to Perryville and the next day "give the enemy battle immediately, rout him, and then move to our support" at Harrodsburg. Bragg still hoped to fight the campaign's climactic battle there, instead of at Perryville.[135]

That evening Buell rested, nursing a sore foot caused by his horse falling on him that afternoon. Despite his pain, he realized that his men had run a part of the Confederate army to ground.

Joseph Wheeler. *Perryville Battlefield State Historic Site.*

On discovering that the enemy was concentrating for battle at Perryville I sent orders on the night of the 7th to General McCook and General Crittenden to march at 3 o'clock the following morning, so as to take position respectively as early as possible on the right and left of the center corps…my intention being to make the attack that day if possible.[136]

Contrary to recent interpretations, no meeting occurred on the night of October 7 to petition for Buell's removal (see Appendix II). However, one group of senior officers did gather that evening. General Sheridan spoke with Brigadier Generals James Jackson and William Terrill and Colonel George Webster, the three senior officers of the 10th Division. Terrill was a Virginian and a West Point graduate who had stayed loyal to the United States; his brother was an officer in the Confederate army. Sheridan and Terrill had a blood feud that went back to their days at the Point and a brawl that had caused Sheridan to miss a year and injured his class standing. They buried the hatchet that evening, and in the ensuing discussion they all agreed on the miniscule chances that all four would be killed the next day. Three of them had less than twenty-four hours to live.[137]

As the armies bedded down on the night of October 7, both Buell and Bragg expected to fight a victorious offensive battle at Perryville in the morning. It was a place neither had expected to meet, but now the armies were poised for the first major encounter in Kentucky since Munfordville, twenty-one days earlier. The next day was Wednesday, October 8, 1862, and would mark one week since the Army of the Ohio left Louisville. Little did either side suspect that the Kentucky Campaign's bloody climax was at hand.

CHAPTER 7

DYING FOR WATER

B y the evening of October 7, 1862, the focus of the Kentucky Campaign had shifted to one of the most historic areas of the state, namely the triangle formed by Harrodsburg to the north, Danville to the southeast and Perryville to the southwest. Approximately ten miles separated each city from the other. The city of Harrodsburg dated from 1774 and was the oldest permanent English settlement west of the Appalachian Mountains. Danville had been founded in the 1780s and was the state's first capital; here also the first constitution of the new Commonwealth of Kentucky had been written. Not far from town was the residence and grave of the state's first governor, Isaac Shelby. Kentucky had started in this region, and it seemed appropriate that its fate would be decided there in 1862.

The city of Perryville numbered about four hundred residents in 1862, and that January had marked its forty-fifth anniversary as a chartered city in Kentucky. The area was settled in the 1770s by Pennsylvanians led by James Harbison, and the locality was first known as Harbison's Station. The settlement's location was determined by the Chaplin River and a natural spring located in a cave near the river's west bank. Indian raids slowed the settlement's growth, but by the early nineteenth century it had grown into a healthy town. On January 17, 1817, the settlement was chartered as a city and named Perryville in honor of Commodore Oliver Hazard Perry, the hero of the 1813 Battle of Lake Erie. Perryville was first located in Mercer County but became part of Boyle County in 1842.

Over the years, Perryville had grown into a regional center for western Boyle County. Four major pikes provided good communication with

Harrodsburg to the northeast, Danville to the east, Lebanon to the southwest and Springfield to the west, while smaller roads serviced the hamlets of Mitchellsburg to the south and Mackville to the northwest. In 1862, Perryville's active commercial district was centered along the Chaplin's west bank, an area known since the 1840s as Merchant's Row. The city also boasted a girls' school, a college, a small seminary, a Masonic hall and many other trappings of Victorian municipal accomplishment. The surrounding area featured many farms of varying sizes, the largest being Henry P. "Squire" Bottom's six hundred acres located on the Mackville Road. Many locals owned a small number of slaves, while several free blacks lived in Perryville itself.[138]

Perryville had so far escaped most of the war. Aside from wagons shuttling between Bardstown and Camp Breckinridge, very little military activity had occurred in the area before the armies arrived in October. As the city realized it was probably about to become a battlefield, the citizens hurriedly packed up and evacuated on the night of October 7 and the early morning of October 8. Several residents tried to wait out the battle in their cellars, but most left town.[139]

As dusk fell on October 7, Hardee deployed his two Left Wing divisions in and around the town with Buckner's division to the west and Anderson's division to the northwest. Cheatham's division of the Right Wing camped a few miles north along the Harrodsburg Road. Buckner's westernmost brigade was a tough all-Arkansas outfit under Brigadier General St. John R. Liddell. Liddell's brigade was initially deployed on Bottom Hill a mile west of town, but he soon realized that the height to his front (known as Peters Hill) commanded the area. An additional bonus was that Doctor's Creek ran along Peters Hill's western edge and was one of the few decent water sources in the area. The Springfield Pike traversed Doctor's Creek before climbing Peters Hill, and any Federal attack would be channeled through that crossing. Holding most of his infantry on Bottom Hill, Liddell sent the 7th Arkansas to occupy Peters Hill and watch for the enemy. General Polk arrived during the night and assumed command of the sixteen thousand Confederate troops in and around Perryville.[140]

West of town in the Federal III Corps lines, General Sheridan's 11th Division camped closest to the enemy on the Springfield Pike. Sheridan was aware of Doctor's Creek, which represented the best water supply he and

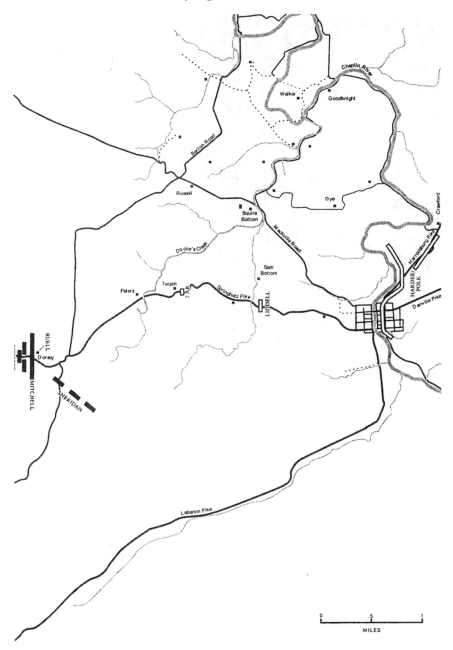

Perryville Battlefield at 1:00 a.m., October 8, 1862, shortly before Sheridan's division moved forward to secure Doctor's Creek and Peters Hill. *Courtesy John P. Walsh Jr.*

St. John Liddell. *Perryville Battlefield State Historic Site.*

his thirsty soldiers had encountered since Bardstown. Indeed, some of his men had snuck beyond Union lines to get water already. Expecting a battle the next day, Sheridan wanted to start with full canteens; he accordingly requested and received permission to secure the creek and the hill beyond.[141]

Sheridan gave the mission to his newest brigade and brigade commander, Colonel Daniel McCook's 36th Brigade. Colonel McCook was the younger brother of the I Corps commander and had raised the 52nd Ohio that summer. All of the 36th Brigade's regiments were new to combat, but they had already impressed Sheridan with their discipline and leadership. Night combat in the Civil War was a perilous business, but a near-full moon would aid visibility. Sheridan and Dan McCook expected their men to give their best.[142]

At 3:00 a.m. on October 8, 1862, the 52nd Ohio moved eastward as skirmishers toward Peters Hill. By 3:30 a.m., the regiment, with the 86th Illinois following in support, had crossed Doctor's Creek via the bridge and started up the slope of Peters Hill. The 7th Arkansas was caught off guard, and after a short but sharp engagement fell back to Bottom Hill. Within an hour after starting, Dan McCook's Federals had control of the water and the

Dying for Water

Philip Sheridan. *Perryville Battlefield State Historic Site.*

hill. As the 52nd's commander later reported, "To the Thirty-sixth Brigade and to the Fifty-second Regiment thus attaches the honor of opening the great and decisive battle of Perryville."[143]

Liddell's Arkansans regrouped and started actively skirmishing with the 36th Brigade to keep them at bay on Peters Hill. The 52nd Ohio was joined by the rest of the brigade, and as dawn broke both sides blazed away at each other no more than four hundred yards apart. Determined to press his advantage, Sheridan moved his other two brigades under Lieutenant Colonel Bernard Laiboldt and Colonel Nicholas Greusel to support Dan McCook atop Peters Hill. Aware that his rookie 24th Wisconsin was participating in its first battle, the long-bearded Greusel explained that the Wisconsinites would be in reserve to start but they might be needed to fight. "I shall expect you to do it," he said. "From what I have seen of you, I know you will do your duty." The 24th did get into the firefight along with the rest of Greusel's men, but suffered only one man killed. The 24th's seventeen-year-old adjutant, Lieutenant Arthur McArthur, quickly made a name for

91

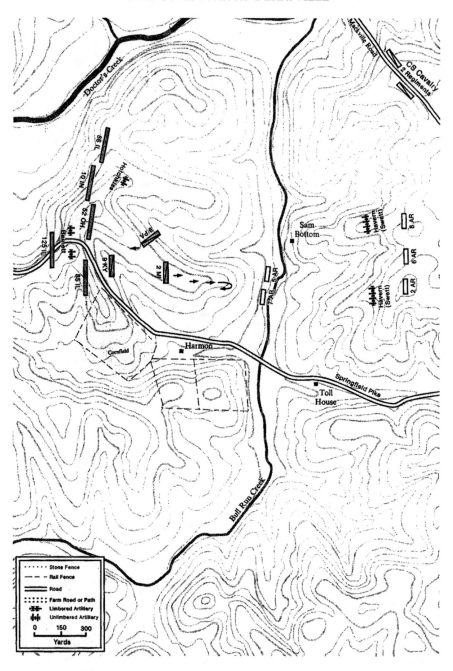

Perryville Battlefield at 8:00 a.m., as both sides battle for Peters Hill and Bottom Hill. *Courtesy John P. Walsh Jr.*

Dying for Water

Nicholas Greusel. *Perryville Battlefield State Historic Site.*

himself for his bravery and steady example during the engagement. It was the start of a great and famous military career for this officer, who after the war changed the spelling of his name to MacArthur; his son Douglas would attain great martial heights in his own right.[144]

In response to the sudden appearance of the Federals and the loss of a water supply, Liddell tried to counterattack with the 5th and 7th Arkansas. "The attempt was promptly and cheerfully made, but the force of the enemy had been increased so largely and suddenly as to force back both lines," reported Liddell. As the Confederates retired, dismounted Federal cavalry attacked from the northwest. The 2nd Michigan and the 9th Pennsylvania quickly drew the fire of Liddell's infantry and artillery and were pinned down.[145]

At this point, Sheridan committed Laiboldt's veteran 2nd and 15th Missouri, both German outfits from St. Louis. Supported by the 44th Illinois, the Missourians formed in a belt of woods atop Peters Hill and attacked directly at the left of Liddell's line. This new threat, coupled with the concentrated fire of Sheridan's divisional artillery on Peters Hill, proved too much for the Confederates. At 10:00 a.m., Buckner ordered Liddell back into Perryville. The Federals took possession of the heights west of town.[146]

Shortly after Sheridan captured Bottom Hill, the last natural obstacle before Perryville proper, General Gilbert rode onto the field. Gilbert was quite concerned that his troops were forward of Peters Hill, and in his usual tactless way he let his feelings be known. As he later wrote, "On inquiry it was discovered that this movement was in consequence of some misunderstanding of orders. General Sheridan was directed to recall [Laiboldt's] brigade, resume his position, and limit himself to its defense until a general advance to attack in force should be ordered." Reluctantly, Sheridan abandoned Bottom Hill and retired his entire division to Peters Hill, where it joined Mitchell's 9th Division, which had arrived on the field in support. Schoepf's 1st Division stayed in the rear near Doctor's Creek.[147]

The engagement over water began the day on a rather bloody note. Sheridan's division left nearly 300 casualties on the field, including 70 Germans of the 2nd Missouri. Greusel's brigade and Laiboldt's brigade both lost approximately 120 men apiece to secure the water and the heights. Liddell sustained 72 casualties for the entire day, the majority occurring on and near Bottom Hill.[148]

The battle for Peters Hill convinced both Hardee and Polk that large numbers of Federal troops were on the field and that Bragg's plan for an attack and disengagement was impractical. Cheatham's division arrived during the morning and was posted to the north of town along the Harrodsburg Pike. Wharton's cavalry scouted the Mackville Road area to the northwest while Wheeler's horsemen watched the Lebanon Pike to the southwest. "At a meeting of the general officers, held about daylight, it was resolved, in view of the great disparity of our forces, to adopt the defensive-offensive, to await the movements of the enemy, and to be guided by events as they were developed," Polk later explained.[149]

The wisdom of Polk's decision was confirmed when blue columns were seen approaching along the Mackville Road and the Lebanon Pike. McCook's I Corps had been on the road starting at 3:00 a.m., and by 10:00 a.m. was approaching the battlefield along the Mackville Road. Near Lebanon, Crittenden's II Corps had been delayed getting into bivouac and was late starting, and only neared Perryville about 11:30 a.m. By lunchtime, fifty-five thousand U.S. troops stood within five miles of Perryville. Yet Buell's intended grand offensive was hopelessly late, so he postponed the Army of the Ohio's attack until dawn on October 9. Both McCook and Crittenden were ordered to deploy near III Corps and reconnoiter.[150]

South of Perryville, Crittenden's twenty thousand men strung out in a rough line of battle behind cavalry commanded by Colonel Edward

Dying for Water

Edward McCook. *Perryville Battlefield State Historic Site.*

McCook, a cousin of Alexander and Daniel. The Union horsemen made contact with Wheeler's cavalry screen but did not press an attack. For his part, Wheeler was content to watch and wait.[151]

Northwest of Perryville, Alexander McCook brought his thirteen thousand men in two divisions on the field via the Mackville Road. The I Corps column was a little mixed up; in the lead was General Rousseau's 3rd Division, but only two of its brigades (led by Colonels William H. Lytle and Leonard Harris) were in their proper place. Anxious to get started, James Jackson's 10th Division was moving before Rousseau's last brigade under John Starkweather could get into line. Starkweather's men now marched at the back of the procession with the corps supply wagons.

As McCook's soldiers approached Perryville, they heard the sound of the Peters Hill engagement in the distance. Many of the 21st Wisconsin's rookies thought the sound came from a thunderstorm, but Sergeant John H. Otto, a veteran of the Prussian army, knew better. "I did know the meaning of it all," he wrote later, "but I kept my peace. Soon enough the men would realize the real cause."[152]

John C. Russell, shown here in the 1880s, was a Unionist whose house became headquarters for Alexander McCook. *Perryville Battlefield State Historic Site.*

With skirmishers in front, Rousseau's lead brigades pressed eastward past where the Benton Road intersected the Mackville Road, a place known as the Dixville Crossroads. As the infantry passed John C. Russell's farmhouse near the intersection, McCook selected the property for his headquarters. Russell was a Unionist, and opened his house to the general and his entourage.[153]

The infantry pressed ahead a mile eastward and finally came to rest atop a ridge (now known as Loomis Heights) about two miles northwest of Perryville. Doctor's Creek ran parallel to and a little bit east of the ridge's eastern face, and just to the southeast stood the barn and house of H.P. Bottom. Lytle deployed his Ohio, Kentucky and Indiana troops astride the Mackville Road overlooking the creek and the Bottom House, while Harris took his Indianans, Ohioans and Wisconsinites north to cover Lytle's left. The 10th and 33rd Ohio moved forward as skirmishers.[154]

The John C. Russell House as seen in 1885. It burned down in the 1960s and not a trace remains today. *Perryville Battlefield State Historic Site.*

Jackson's all-rookie 10th Division arrived shortly after Rousseau placed his troops, and he quickly tied in to the I Corps deployment. His men were tired and thirsty; most had not had breakfast due to their commander's haste. Leaving George Webster's brigade at the crossroads as corps reserve, Jackson took Terrill's three thousand soldiers and eight cannon north along the Benton Road to a promontory known as Open Knob, which covered Harris's left and offered good observation of the surrounding area. By noon, four of the five I Corps brigades were in place, and Starkweather's men were approaching.[155]

About 10:00 a.m., as Liddell broke off at Bottom Hill and I Corps came into view, General Bragg rode onto the scene from Harrodsburg. He was angry not to find a Confederate attack in progress. He also refused to believe that Buell's entire army was present or approaching the field. Overruling any objections from Polk and Hardee, Bragg ordered an immediate offensive against the most exposed and accessible part of the Union army: McCook's I Corps, now deployed two miles northwest of Perryville along the Mackville Road.[156]

Bragg planned to hit McCook using a simple echelon attack. Leaving only three brigades (Colonel Samuel Powell's troops of Anderson's division and Preston Smith's Tennesseans from Cheatham's division, plus Wheeler's cavalry, numbering 3,500 men all told) in and around Perryville to watch the forty-two thousand men of II and III Corps, the remaining thirteen thousand Confederates would strike McCook's thirteen thousand Federals northwest of town. Bragg's units would attack stair-step fashion in echelon from north to south, building gradual pressure against I Corps and breaking the Federal line. The Dixville Crossroads was a key objective; if it fell to the Confederacy, McCook's corps would be surrounded and subject to annihilation. Jump-off time was set at 2:00 p.m.[157]

Getting to McCook would be difficult, for the Chaplin River ran parallel to the Confederate front. The drought made it easily fordable for men, but wagons and artillery needed roads to cross. Buckner's division followed the Mackville Road one mile northwest and stopped just out of Lytle's view. Anderson's detached brigades in the center moved via farm lanes and across country to opposite Harris's positions. Cheatham's men had the toughest path, via the narrow Dug Road and into a 270-degree turn in the Chaplin called Walker's Bend. Wharton's cavalry scouted the area but reported only the presence of Harris's and Lytle's brigades. Federal cannon on Loomis Heights soon drove the Confederate troopers to ground, while Southern artillery dueled their Federal counterparts.[158]

As Cheatham's men moved into position, on the banks of the Chaplin they ran into skirmishers of the 33rd Ohio. After trading a few volleys, the Confederates deployed and pushed the Federals back. One of the Ohioans later described the battle: "Our regiment was sent out on the left to prevent a surprise from that direction...We had not been there long when a regiment of cavalry made its appearance on our front and a regiment of infantry on our left. We fired one round, killed their flag bearer and a few other of their men and then we retreated back to our regiment, the rebels following close to our heels." As the 33rd rallied and fell back toward Harris's main

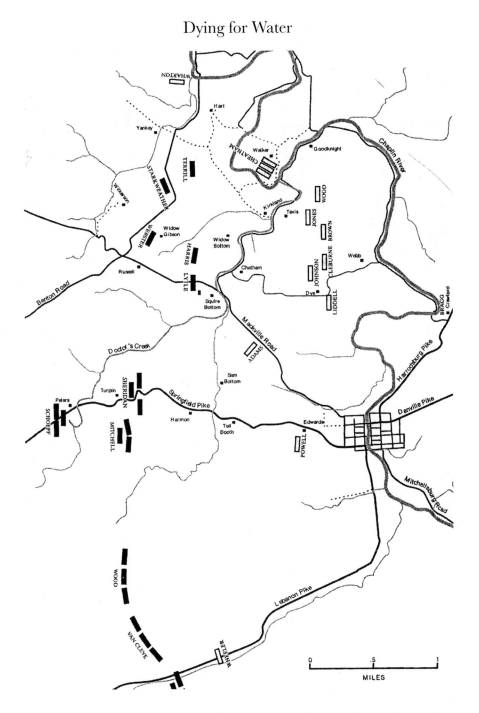

Perryville Battlefield at 2:00 p.m., just before the opening of Bragg's offensive. *Courtesy John P. Walsh Jr.*

Benjamin Cheatham. *Perryville Battlefield State Historic Site.*

line, nobody saw the regiment's colonel, Oscar Moore, fall wounded. The regiment's color-bearer suffered the same fate, and both men and the flag were taken by the Confederates.[159]

As the appointed hour of 2:00 p.m. approached, Cheatham deployed his six thousand men. He commanded three brigades under Brigadier Generals George Maney, Alexander P. Stewart and Daniel Donelson, all of the Volunteer State. Every regiment in the division was made up of Tennessee veterans except for the rookie 41st Georgia. Based on his best information, his entire division stood beyond the Federal left flank; Cheatham decided to strike with Donelson's troops and use his remaining brigades as a reserve to exploit any success.[160]

Cheatham's men moved up from Walker's Bend to their assigned positions using the terrain and woods for cover and concealment. Confederate artillery continued to shell Union positions at Loomis Heights. General Donelson deployed his Tennesseans, aware that the start of the battle hinged on his attack. At 2:00 p.m. all was ready, so he gave permission for his men to move ahead. Little did he know that his order was starting five sustained hours of intense combat that would push both sides to their limit.

After a midday lull, the Battle of Perryville was picking up again in earnest.

CHAPTER 8

BRAGG ATTACKS

While Bragg's Confederates moved into position for their attack, at 1:30 p.m. Colonel John Starkweather's 28th Brigade arrived at the Dixville Crossroads. Colonel Starkweather was a militia officer who had lived in Milwaukee since 1851. His brigade represented the final element of McCook's corps to arrive, and they were here none too soon.

Starkweather parked the I Corps supply trains at the Dixville Crossroads and tried to figure out his next move. None of McCook's or Rousseau's staff officers was there to guide him as to where to go or what to do. Harris's and Lytle's brigades of Rousseau's division were deployed at Loomis Heights a mile to the east, supported by Colonel George P. Webster's brigade from Jackson's division. The rest of the 10th Division was grouped around the Open Knob to the left of Rousseau's line. Between the Open Knob and the Dixville Crossroads were two more ridges running generally parallel with the Mackville Road. Heavy shelling to the front indicated that the battle was about to get underway.[161]

Faced with this dilemma, Starkweather made a key decision on his own. As he wrote later, "Finding the troops already engaged well on the right, center, and left and thinking the extreme left position most accessible and from appearances one that should be held at all hazards, I placed my command at once." Heading northeast along the Benton Road, the 24th Illinois deployed in the fields south of the road, linking with Harris's brigade. The 79th Pennsylvania then took position in a woodline to the left of the 24th, with its left flank resting on the roadway. The 1st Wisconsin and the brigade's two batteries posted on an eminence north of the Benton Road,

John C. Starkweather. *Perryville Battlefield State Historic Site.*

soon to be known ever after as Starkweather Hill. In front of Starkweather Hill sprawled a large cornfield and beyond that was the Open Knob. The 21st Wisconsin was held in reserve behind the hill.[162]

General Rousseau appeared as this deployment was being completed. He approved Starkweather's initiative, and later commented that "Colonel Starkweather...had the good sense...to fall in on our left, and I found his brigade on the very spot where it was most needed." Rousseau did make one significant change to the brigade's dispositions, ordering the 21st forward into the corn in front of Starkweather Hill.[163]

As the 21st Wisconsin moved into its new position, less than a mile away General Donelson rode over to his lead regiments, the 15th and 16th Tennessee. The 16th's commander, Colonel John Savage, was an old U.S. Army veteran and a notoriously prickly officer. He openly disrespected both Donelson and Cheatham, and had previously been on report for insubordination. As Donelson and Savage stood at a woodline and surveyed the terrain in front

Daniel Donelson. *Perryville Battlefield State Historic Site.*

of them, Donelson pointed to the only Federal battery visible—Captain Samuel Harris's of Webster's brigade, posted near the Dixville Crossroads—and marked it as the Tennesseans' objective. Overriding Savage's strong objections, Donelson three times told Savage to attack. Finally, at 2:00 p.m., the perturbed colonel formed his men and led them forward in a frontal attack toward Webster's command.[164]

The 16th and 15th joined together and moved west with the 38th Tennessee in support. Advancing with their left along a small creek, the Tennesseans disappeared into a small dip and then climbed up into a bowl formed by a wooded ridge to the north, an open ridge to the south and a ridge with a cabin (owned by the widow Mary Jane Gibson) to the west. At first the attack went well, but as the men rose out of the bowl they began to realize that they were in a terrible trap. Ahead of them stood the three thousand rookie Federals and six cannon of Webster's brigade, to the left (south) was Leonard Harris's veterans and on the Confederate northern (right) flank the veteran 24th Illinois of Starkweather's brigade had just taken up position. In addition, for the first time the Confederates detected the presence of Jackson's troops on the Open Knob. The Union troops all announced their presence with shells and bullets; an observer later recorded, "As the 16th Tennessee approached the lowest point of this depression the enemy opened a murderous fire upon them with musketry and artillery from right, left and centre. The ranks of the 16th Regt. were mowed down at a fearful rate, and the 15th Regt., also suffered severely. The ranks closed up, and the brigade pressed onward in the charge."[165]

Despite severe fire from three sides, the Tennesseans kept going. They pushed to within 150 yards of Webster's position before being pinned down by the concentrated Union fire. As the battle swirled toward her home, the Widow Gibson grabbed her three sons (ages ten, eight and five) and hid below the cabin's floorboards for the rest of the day. Meanwhile, Rousseau shifted several of Harris's and Starkweather's regiments to help stem the tide. By 2:30 p.m., most of Donelson's men had been driven all the way back to their jump-off positions.[166]

The failure of Donelson's attack unhinged Cheatham's plan, for it demonstrated that the Federal northern flank was not where the Confederates thought it to be. Instead of using Maney's and Stewart's excellent brigades as an exploitation force, Cheatham was forced to redeploy them to make a frontal attack against the northern part of the Union line. Maney's Tennessee and Georgia troops would lead the assault, with Stewart's men providing support.

Cheatham's new target was the Open Knob, topped by eight cannon in a provisional battery commanded by Lieutenant Charles Parsons. Three thousand infantry of William Terrill's brigade were posted atop the hill and along its sides. This battle represented Terrill's first command of infantry, and most of his men were in action for the first time. Terrill's division commander, James Jackson, was atop the hill and directing the battle from astride his horse. At the base of Open Knob stood a rail fence, which stood about one hundred yards from the crest. Beyond the fence, approximately three hundred yards of rolling open ground rose to a wooded ridge where Maney's men had formed for the attack.[167]

Maney could see the large numbers of Union troops atop Open Knob, so the general decided to advance with artillery support. Lieutenant William

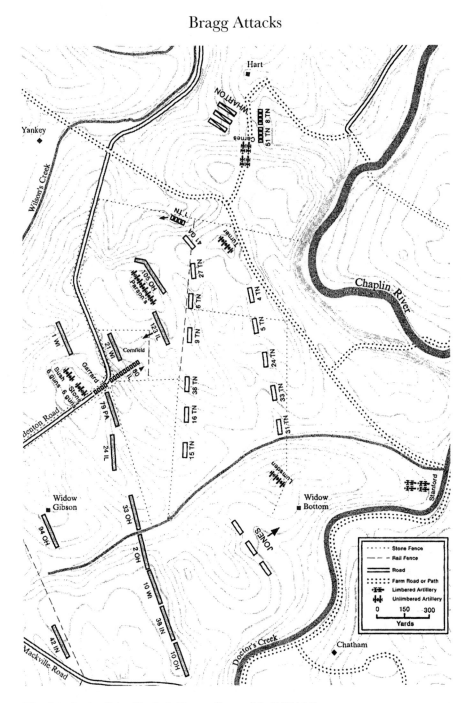

The fight for the Open Knob, 3:00 p.m. *Courtesy John P. Walsh Jr.*

George Maney. *Perryville Battlefield State Historic Site.*

Turner's Mississippi battery of four cannon deployed on Maney's right and commenced shelling Open Knob with canister. Meanwhile, Maney's infantry emerged from the woods in one long line. Captain Percival Oldershaw of Jackson's staff described the Federal reaction: "No sooner was this seen by General Terrill and Lieutenant Parsons, then directing the fire of the guns, than they changed the direction of the fire, and opened at short range (about 90 yards) on the flank of the enemy with grape with deadly accuracy."[168]

The Confederates swept ahead with the 41st Georgia on the right and the 6th and 9th Tennessee to the left. The 1st and 27th Tennessee remained in reserve. Federal fire grew heavier, especially as Terrill fed the 123rd Illinois into the fight. Finally, Maney's attack stalled out at the fence, "at which time it seemed impossible for humanity to go farther, such was the havoc and destruction that had taken place in [our] ranks," according to Colonel George Porter of the 6th Tennessee. The Confederates took shelter behind the rails, unable to go forward and unwilling to go back. The fight for the Open Knob settled down into a stalemate.[169]

The Confederate advance had come to a standstill, but the ensuing firefight had a profound impact on the battle's course. As the 123rd Illinois maneuvered in the face of Confederate fire, General Jackson turned to one of his staffers and remarked, "I'll be damned if this is not getting rather particular." Suddenly, two Confederate bullets ripped into his chest, knocking him from the saddle. Captain Oldershaw rushed to him, and later described what he saw: "I found him on his back, struggling to speak, but unable to do so. He died in a few moments." At a stroke, the Union troops on Open Knob had lost their most experienced infantry officer.[170]

General Terrill was now thrust into command of both Open Knob and the 10th Division. Faced with this sudden rush of responsibility, he fell back on his roots in the artillery and spent much of his time directing the fire of Parsons's eight cannon while the infantry blazed away on their own. Occasionally, he would send an infantry regiment down the hill to try and drive the Confederates away, but the new troops always withered under the enemy's volleys.[171]

On the Confederate side, calm leadership held the situation together. General Maney saw his brigade waver and went forward to steady his men. He walked back and forth along the battle line, inspiring the men with his courage in the face of Union fire. On Maney's orders, the 1st Tennessee began moving around Terrill's northern flank. Maney was preparing to lead a rush at Parsons's cannon when the rookie 105th Ohio started down the slope toward his men. The 105th's Private Josiah Ayre was in his first battle since joining the army the previous August, and he described what happened to his outfit:

> By some reason or another we could not form into a proper line, and after going through several maneuvers in order to do so we became mixed and confused, not knowing what our officers were saying. Finally we were ordered to load and fire the best we could, although I could not see a rebel at the time on account of the shape of the ground. Some of [our men] commenced firing, however, and I with some others marched forward, ahead of the regiment, so that we could get sight of them...I repeated this 2 or 3 times before we were ordered to fall back, with the enemy not 15 rods ahead of us. By this time every man seemed to be looking out for himself as we were all broken up. For my part, I could not tell whether we had any regiment or not.

Private William Howard
Co. "K" 105th Ohio
Killed in Action

William Howard of the 105th Ohio fought his first battle at Perryville. He died on the front slope of the Open Knob. *Perryville Battlefield State Historic Site.*

In a matter of minutes, Maney's men shattered the Ohioans with well-directed fire from the fence. Ayre and many of his comrades were hit as they fell back up the hill. The 105th Ohio represented the last unit that Terrill would throw away on the front slope of Open Knob.[172]

As the 105th broke, General Maney motioned his men over the fence. "Every man was instantly on his feet, and I don't suppose that twelve hundred men ever have made such a yell before," recalled one of Maney's staff officers. The Confederates rushed up the hill and swarmed over Parsons's cannon in hand-to-hand fighting. Both General Terrill and Lieutenant Parsons had to be physically dragged from the guns to avoid capture, but seven of the eight cannon fell to the Southerners. By 3:30 p.m., Maney's troops had achieved their first objective, but more work remained: John Starkweather's veteran brigade loomed ahead.[173]

The twelve guns on Starkweather Hill immediately opened fire, and Open Knob soon became unhealthy for the Confederates. Stewart's reserve brigade now advanced on Maney's left, and with this momentum Maney's men pushed down the Open Knob's back slope toward the cornfield that held the 21st Wisconsin.

Bragg Attacks

The 21st was an untried regiment, so new that it had not yet received its battle flag. The unit had also only drilled together three times before this battle. Despite its newness, the regiment already had a feisty reputation, thanks to the slave episode in Bloomfield a few days earlier. Colonel Sweet had taken ill that morning, so the unit deployed for its first fight under Major Friedrich Schumacher, a German immigrant and veteran of the Prussian army. Unfortunately, the Wisconsinites could see nothing on account of the eight-foot-tall corn blocking their view. Federal fugitives retreating from the Open Knob fight had disrupted the unit's line, and Major Schumacher ordered the men to "keep cool and not to fire too high when the order was given."[174]

Maney's troops moved toward the 21st's front, while Stewart's veterans approached the unit's right and right rear. Their battle flags loomed above the corn. As the 21st's James Pillar later remembered, "Some one gave the order and we up and let fly." Two volleys rang out from the 21st at point-blank range, dropping Confederate officers and men alike. Leader losses now started to blunt the Confederate combat edge. The 41st Georgia and 5th Tennessee both lost their commanders to wounds, while the 9th Tennessee lost every company commander in and around the corn.[175]

The two volleys were all the Wisconsinites could manage before the Confederates crashed in on them. Hand-to-hand combat broke out as both sides grappled for possession of the cornfield. Major Schumacher went down with two wounds and lay dying behind his horse. Captain George Bentley of the 21st's Company H emptied his revolver into the oncoming Confederates, killed one with his sword and died after shooting another with a captured pistol. One Wisconsinite described how the bullets flew "as thick as rain." Colonel Sweet came from his ambulance to take command and almost immediately suffered a wound that put him out of action. Within minutes, the 21st turned into a fleeing mass of men running back toward Starkweather Hill. Some men rallied at the foot of the hill and made a brief stand before falling back to the safety of Starkweather's cannon. Maney's and Stewart's Confederate infantries followed in close pursuit.[176]

By 3:45 p.m., most of Cheatham's division was bearing down on the 1,500 men in Starkweather's three veteran regiments. Donelson's men had renewed the attack and were pressing on the 24th Illinois of Starkweather's brigade. The 24th, a predominantly German outfit from Chicago, fought hard but was pushed back into a position bent at right angles to the 79th

Colonel Charles A. McDaniel
41st Georga Infantry
Mortally Wounded at Perryville

Colonel Charles McDaniel led
his rookie 41ˢᵗ Georgia into battle
for the first time at Perryville. He
was mortally wounded in front
of Starkweather Hill. *Perryville
Battlefield State Historic Site.*

Pennsylvania. The Illinoisans and Pennsylvanians combined with parts of Webster's brigade to halt Donelson's Tennesseans again.[177]

Maney's and Stewart's troops swarmed up Starkweather Hill as Colonel Starkweather turned to his men and shouted, "Now, my brave 1ˢᵗ Wisconsin, do your duty!" Sergeant Elias Hoover of the 1ˢᵗ recalled how the "rebels came in solid column to take the battery, and we were ordered to rise and fire. The old 1ˢᵗ would not waver, and the fight was hand-to-hand over those cannon." The 1ˢᵗ Wisconsin successfully defended the guns from this first attempt. The Confederates fell back to regroup.[178]

Maney's and Stewart's men reformed and attacked again up the front of Starkweather Hill. This second charge wilted under the fire of the cannon and Wisconsinites in front and the 79ᵗʰ Pennsylvania on the flank. Colonel Starkweather was in the thickest of the fighting, shouting to his men to "Give 'em hell!" "The 1ˢᵗ Wisconsin and 79ᵗʰ Pennsylvania [took] the brunt and although badly used up we made them *skedaddle*," crowed Captain William Mitchell of the 1ˢᵗ Wisconsin. Frustrated again, the Confederates fell back to the foot of the hill.[179]

Bragg Attacks

It was now about 4:15 p.m., and a short lull settled over the action. Both sides took the opportunity to survey the situation. Starkweather Hill had proven impregnable to attacks from the front, so General Maney decided to use the 1st Tennessee to flank the Union line. The regiment's Colonel Hume Feild had the same thought and set about getting into position. Colonel Starkweather observed this movement from atop the hill and realized that he might not be able to hold back a third Confederate charge. Looking south along Rousseau's battle line, he saw Federal troops giving way. If Starkweather's men stayed where they were, the 28th Brigade might be surrounded and defeated. The situation was critical. It was time to move.[180]

CHAPTER 9

THE CONFEDERATES
SLIP THE FANG

W hat Colonel Starkweather saw as he looked south was Hardee's Confederate Left Wing attacking the Federal positions overlooking Doctor's Creek and the Bottom House. While Cheatham's men engaged Terrill and Starkweather to the north, other Confederate units were swinging into action as part of the echelon attack.

The second part of the echelon got underway about 3:00 p.m., while Maney's troops were pinned along the fence in front of Open Knob. South of Cheatham's division stood two brigades from Anderson's division under Colonel Thomas Jones of Mississippi and Brigadier General John C. Brown of Tennessee. General Brown was an experienced infantry commander with a good brigade, while the thirty-year-old Jones was filling in for General Anderson and had never commanded any force larger than a regiment before this battle. Jones's three inexperienced Mississippi regiments were deployed just south of Donelson's men with Brown's Florida and Mississippi units to their left. Significantly, General Anderson never visited this end of the field, preferring instead to remain with the other elements of his division on the Springfield Pike. He also failed to designate a single commander for the two detached brigades, so they operated more or less independently during the battle.[181]

Leonard Harris's 9th Brigade of Rousseau's division stood opposite Jones and Brown. Except for the rookie 94th Ohio Infantry, the rest of Harris's Ohioans, Indianans and Wisconsinites were all veterans. Harris's men had been on the field for several hours and were prepared to defend their position. They were supported by Captain Peter Simonson's six-gun 5th

Indiana Battery. Simonson's artillery and the 33rd Ohio of this brigade had already engaged the Confederates during the day, and several of Harris's regiments had helped pin and repulse Donelson's initial charge.[182]

The terrain in front of Harris's line was some of the most intricate on the battlefield. An east–west crest separated Donelson's axis of attack from Jones's path, while three north–south ridges paralleled the Union battle line. Harris's men occupied the westernmost crest, which was open, while the tree-lined eastern ridge belonged to the Confederacy. Between the two forces a narrow rise reached just high enough to create an optical illusion that the enemy was only on the next ridge over. In the valley fronting Harris's position was a small cornfield and a sinkhole.

Shortly before Jones's men jumped off, Captain Charles Lumsden's Alabama Battery unlimbered at the edge of the woods and started an intense preparatory bombardment of Harris's position. Simonson's guns replied and succeeded in knocking out one of Lumsden's cannon. Yet the optical illusion ate up most of the two thousand rounds the Alabamians expended that day, as much of their fired ammunition ended up merely plowing into the eastern face of the middle rise.[183]

About 3:00 p.m., Jones's three regiments advanced out of the woods in line abreast. Most of his men carried outmoded smoothbore muskets except the men of Company K of the 27th Mississippi, who were equipped with Enfield rifles, so they preceded the infantry lines as skirmishers. It was this company's commander, Captain John Sale, who first perceived something was amiss with this attack. As the brigade advanced toward the middle rise, Sale's men were the first to reach it. One of Company K's men described it as "a precipice fully thirty feet high." Sale halted his men and reported his find back to the main line. "Forward skirmishers!" was the response. Company K led the brigade over the middle rise. As his men topped the crest, Colonel Jones abandoned them to hide in safety.[184]

Suddenly, the Mississippians burst into full view of the Federals, who were barely 150 yards away. Harris's men were startled and impressed by the determination of Jones's attack. "With closed column and the rebel yell, which we then heard for the first time, they came like veterans and the onslaught was terrible," remembered an Ohioan. The Mississippians repeatedly tried to continue over the middle rise despite point-blank fire from Union infantry and artillery. Sophronius Landt of the 10th Wisconsin

The Confederates Slip the Fang

Thomas Jones. *Perryville Battlefield State Historic Site.*

recalled that "soon the solid gray lines as far as we could see began to come steadily down the slope toward us. Meanwhile, our batteries…were pouring a heavy fire of shot and shell into them and making wide gaps into their ranks. But these gaps were quickly closed, and on they came until an effective range for musketry was reached." The Union fire proved too much and the Confederates could not advance farther.[185]

After twenty minutes it was all over as the dazed survivors of Jones's brigade fled for the safety of Confederate lines. Half of the 34th Mississippi lay dead or wounded on the field; only one officer of that regiment escaped unscathed. The casualty rates for the other two regiments also approached 50 percent. Leaderless and confused, Jones's rookies were out of the fight and useless for the rest of the day.[186]

As the Mississippians broke down in front of Harris's men, John C. Brown ordered his three regiments forward about 3:30 p.m. His brigade had sheltered in the valley of Doctor's Creek, and at Brown's command they started enthusiastically toward Harris's Federals. Some of the units got out of alignment, and Brown "cussed us for being too quick," according to the 3rd Florida's Lieutenant John Inglis. "Dress up or you will be cut to pieces in such order," the general warned.[187]

This pause was fortuitous, for it gave General Brown a chance to survey the battlefield while his three regiments—1st and 3rd Florida and 41st Mississippi—straightened themselves out. Witnessing the shattered remnants of Jones's brigade spilling to the rear, Brown realized that his brigade might easily suffer the same fate. He also understood that if his attack failed, the Confederate center would be left wide open for a Federal counterattack that could drive a wedge between Cheatham's troops to the north and Buckner's division to the south. Brown needed to guard the center and hold the line together.

Seeing that his men had corrected their alignment, Brown renewed the advance. As the Confederates came out of the woods, the Federals greeted them with "a severe fire of musketry and shells," according to the 1st Florida's colonel, William Miller. As his men advanced toward the rise where Jones's troops had come to grief, Brown ordered a halt. Spreading his men out along the top of the crest, his entire brigade began trading fire with Harris's Federals, who replied in kind.[188]

Brown's excellent command decision delivered his brigade to precisely the right time and place to do the most good. For the next forty-five minutes both sides lay prone and blazed away at each other as best they could. Confederate rifle fire soon forced Simonson's battery to retire; its place was taken by the 94th Ohio. The Federals had an easy time of it in this fight: according to a Wisconsinite, "we had been well drilled in this particular [prone] method of fighting and could load and fire about as fast as if standing."[189]

But the firefight could not continue indefinitely, and by 4:00 p.m., both sides were running low on ammunition. The need for bullets was especially acute on the Federal side, for Harris's men had already been engaged earlier against the brigades of Donelson and Jones. Colonel Miller of the 1st Florida recalled, "Our officers passed along the line, cutting the cartridge boxes from the bodies of the dead and receiving them from the suffering wounded." Brown's men finally received a new ammunition supply that enabled them to keep up their fire. On the Federal side, the men also searched the wounded and dead for cartridges, but their supply wagons were located a mile west

Some of Leonard Harris's disciplined soldiers. These men from the 38th Indiana helped hold McCook's center with no ammunition. *Perryville Battlefield State Historic Site.*

at the Dixville Crossroads and out of reach in time. Entire regiments soon ran out of ammunition, and officers ordered the men to fix bayonets and lay down under the Confederate bullets. It was a supreme test of discipline to lie on the ridge taking fire with no way to reply. Colonel Harris later described how his men endured this trial: "Without a round of ammunition, under a heavy fire in front and an enfilading fire from the artillery, they held their position for twenty-five minutes." The fighting in the center settled into bloody stalemate.[190]

With the center in stasis, the last chance for the Confederates to break McCook's line was the southernmost part of the echelon, composed of Buckner's strong division and Brigadier General Daniel Adams's Louisiana brigade of Anderson's division. Their mission was to attack west along the Mackville Road, smash the Union troops at the Bottom House and push one mile west to the Dixville Crossroads. The road was defended by Colonel William Lytle's brigade of Kentuckians, Indianans and Ohioans, supported by Captain Cyrus Loomis's six-gun Battery A of the 1st Michigan Light Artillery. To reach the Federal line, the Confederates needed to advance five hundred yards down a long slope in full view of the enemy, cross Doctor's Creek around the Bottom House and finally climb one hundred yards up Loomis Heights to Lytle's position.

Buckner decided to attack up the road in column of brigades. Brigadier General Bushrod Johnson's brigade took the lead, followed by Patrick Cleburne's veteran outfit. Brigadier General S.A.M. "Sam" Wood's troops shifted to support Brown's men. St. John Liddell's brigade brought up the rear.[191]

About 3:30 p.m., as Cheatham's men captured Open Knob and Brown first engaged Harris, Bushrod Johnson ordered his brigade forward. Almost immediately, the movement got out of hand. At the last minute the Confederate axis of advance had been changed, and only part of Johnson's regiments received word of the new direction. His formation broke up as different regiments slalomed about the battlefield according to how they had been ordered to march. Meanwhile, Loomis's guns rained shot and shell on the Confederates.[192]

As Johnson and Buckner worked to straighten out the muddled Tennesseans, suddenly artillery fire flayed them from their left rear. The 44th and 25th Tennessee promptly wheeled left and charged the guns. The 44th's

The Confederates Slip the Fang

colonel, John Fulton, recalled, "We charged rapidly up the hill with fixed bayonets to silence and take the battery on our left, and having gained the top of the hill we found it to be the Washington Artillery, and immediately reported to them that they had been playing upon their own men, when the firing ceased." The artillerists had been shelling Lytle's men when the Confederate infantry got in the way.[193]

Finally, Johnson's troops reformed and continued their advance toward Doctor's Creek and the H.P. Bottom House beyond. This section of the creek featured a deep valley with steep banks, in places sheer cliffs forty feet high with stone retaining walls. Lytle had given permission to the 42nd Indiana to collect water from the creek before the battle, and the men were in the creek bed scouring the "few scum-covered puddles" they could find, according to the unit's major. Their weapons were stacked on the bank and the Indianans were in no position to mount a defense.[194]

Johnson's Tennesseans quickly overran the helpless 42nd Indiana. Many Federals were struck trying to climb out of the creek, and some twenty-five men suffered capture. The rest broke and fled for the safety of Lytle's line. In fifteen minutes the 42nd sustained over 25 percent casualties and was temporarily ruined as a unit.[195]

The Confederates swept across the creek and into the teeth of Lytle's defenses. North of the Mackville Road stood Loomis's cannon and the 10th Ohio, while the 3rd Ohio and 15th Kentucky (U.S.) overlooked the Bottom House south of the road. All three infantry regiments were veterans, while the rookie 88th Indiana stood back in reserve. The 3rd's colonel, John Beatty, described Johnson's approach:

> *They advanced under cover of a house on the side hill, and having reached a point one hundred and fifty yards distant, deployed behind a stone fence* [ten yards up the hill from the Bottom House]. *In this position… the Third rose and delivered its first volley. For a time, I do not know how long thereafter, it seemed as if all hell had broken loose; the air was filled with hissing balls; shells were exploding continuously, and the noise of the guns was deafening.*

The Ohioans' fire was later described by the 37th Tennessee's commander as "an almost overwhelming storm of lead." The 10th Ohio joined in with

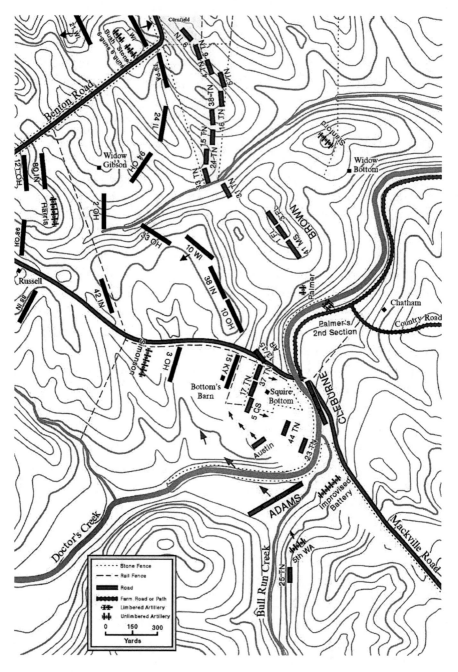

McCook's center and right, 4:00 p.m. *Courtesy John P. Walsh Jr.*

the 3rd, and Johnson's men became pinned along the stone wall near the Bottom House.[196]

About 3:45 p.m., Buckner's next brigade, Patrick Cleburne's veteran outfit, came onto the scene in support of Johnson's beleaguered command. Cleburne's men had fought in the Battle of Richmond and were wearing captured Union equipment, including blue trousers. Cleburne's men hustled under fire to the bed of Doctor's Creek, where the general detached the 13th/15th Arkansas Consolidated Infantry to support Johnson's troops at the stone wall. The Arkansans arrived none too soon, for the Tennesseans were running short of ammunition and had to withdraw. Unwilling to give up the stone wall, Cleburne moved his whole brigade forward as Johnson's men pulled back.[197]

Atop the hill, Beatty's 3rd Ohio also ran short of ammunition and was relieved by the Louisville-based 15th Kentucky. The 15th's 517 men stood atop the hill and traded fire with the thousands of Confederates at the stone wall below; 9 color-bearers were shot down and the regiment's lieutenant colonel and major were both killed. The 15th's commander, Colonel Curran Pope, also suffered a wound but remained in command. He was seen by the unit's adjutant "moving from man to man, patting them on the back, cheering and encouraging them to fight to the end. Such courage could not but inspire them with determination to stand to the last." Just to the right of the battle line stood H.P. Bottom's large barn; shellfire set it ablaze, killing many wounded of both sides that had crawled there for safety. The Kentuckians held firm until they ran low on ammunition and traded places with the 3rd Ohio.[198]

It was now about 4:00 p.m., and Buckner cast about for a way to break the deadlock at the Bottom House. He found Daniel Adams's experienced brigade of Louisiana troops supporting the Washington Artillery to the left of his division. They were in a perfect position to sweep around the Federal flank and slip a fatal fang into McCook's line. Buckner explained his plan and set them in motion. Using folds in the ground for shelter, Adams deployed his 1,900 men at right angles to the 3rd Ohio and 15th Kentucky. Shortly before 4:15 p.m. he ordered his men to advance.[199]

Adams's attack put the 3rd Ohio and 15th Kentucky in a difficult spot. The 15th's Pope turned part of his regiment to face the Louisianans, while the remainder dueled with Cleburne's men. Beatty shifted the 3rd Ohio to face south and ordered his men to fix bayonets and charge. This movement was barely underway when events overtook the two regiments.[200]

At the stone wall, Cleburne was preparing an attack of his own. Adams's onslaught was the signal for his veterans to head over the wall and hit Lytle's front. His effort was victorious thanks to some innovative tactics:

> *I now advanced in line of battle, my skirmishers ten paces in front of the line and carrying the battle-flags of the regiments. As we ascended the hill we were fired into by our own artillery in the rear. Several of our men were killed and wounded, and we had to fall back. I sent an aide to stop this battery. I can only account for this blunder from the fact that most of our men had on blue Federal pants. We again advanced in the same order. The moment our flags, carried by the line of skirmishers, appeared above the crest of the hill, the enemy, supposing our line of battle was in view, emptied their guns at the line of skirmishers. Before they could reload our true line of battle was upon them; they instantly broke and fled, exposed to a deadly fire.*

Under pressure from the front and right, Lytle's entire brigade gave way. "After a short but spirited contest we dislodged and drove them before us. They fled in great disorder, panic, and confusion, throwing their arms and equipment away as they fled," reported General Adams. Colonel Lytle came forward to try and rally his men but fell with a serious head wound. He was left on the field to be captured by the Confederates.[201]

Lytle's collapse unhinged Harris's line and forced him to retire under pressure from Wood's and Brown's Confederates. The Federals fell back in good order, covered by those units that had managed to find ammunition. Harris led his men westward looking for a good place to make a stand.[202]

By 4:30 p.m., McCook's entire line was recoiling under Confederate pressure. On the left, Starkweather prepared to abandon Starkweather Hill; in the center, Leonard Harris's men sought escape from the Confederates pushing on their rear and right; Lytle's Federals on the right had collapsed. Meanwhile, Polk and Hardee urged their men to greater exertions, hoping to turn the Union retreat into a rout. The battle balanced on a knife edge; the Confederate objective, the Dixville Crossroads, was a mile away.

McCook's corps was now fighting for its existence. His men needed time and space to recover their equilibrium and blunt the Confederate attacks. At this critical time, several leaders stepped forward and acted to save I Corps from destruction.

CHAPTER 10

CLIMAX AT THE DIXVILLE CROSSROADS

While McCook's corps battled the Confederates, the Army of the Ohio's commander enjoyed a quiet afternoon not far away. General Buell, sore from his fall on October 7, remained at his headquarters two miles to the south at the James Dorsey House. The Dorsey House was surrounded by rolling terrain, which helped shield sounds from that location. West and south winds also carried noises away from headquarters. All of this combined to ensure that General Buell did not know until late in the afternoon that a major battle was in progress.

All Buell heard, as he described later, was "a sudden increase of cannonading at 2 o'clock...but as the firing as suddenly subsided, and no report came to me, I had ceased to think of the occurrence." In the middle of the afternoon, Generals Buell and Gilbert ate an unhurried lunch. Colonel John M. Harlan of the 10th Kentucky camped near the Dorsey House that day, and in a postwar letter he confirmed how oblivious the Army of the Ohio's headquarters remained: "I was within one hundred yards of Buell's headquarters during the whole time of the battle...I heard no firing from the direction of the battlefield, and if I did not hear it, Buell could not have done so."[203]

About 4:00 p.m., one of Alexander McCook's staff officers rode up to Buell and reported that I Corps "had been seriously engaged for several hours and that the right and left of that corps were being turned and severely pressed," as Buell recalled. McCook also asked for help. Stunned by this news and its implications, Buell ordered two brigades from Gilbert's III Corps north to assist. About 4:30 p.m., Colonel Michael Gooding's brigade of Mitchell's

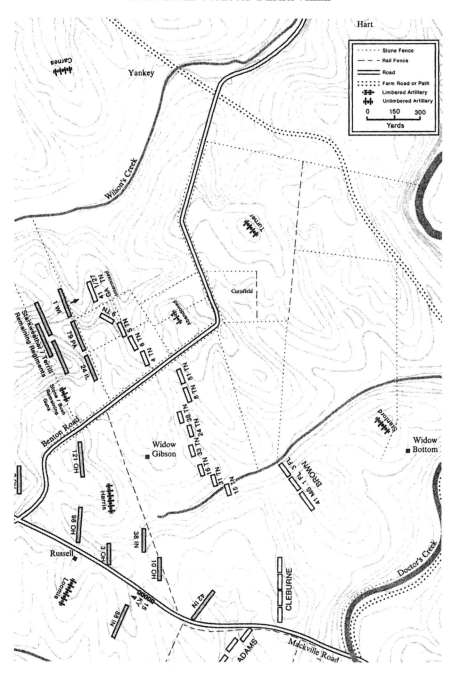

The Dixville Crossroads, 4:45 p.m. *Courtesy John P. Walsh Jr.*

division and Colonel James B. Steedman's brigade of Schoepf's division started to march north toward the Dixville Crossroads, Gooding's brigade in the lead. They were due at the intersection by 5:30 p.m.[204]

Meanwhile, I Corps struggled to survive under Confederate pressure. Terrill's and Lytle's brigades were shattered, while Harris's men desperately sought supplies and a good defensive position. Starkweather's regiments on the left were in good order but about to pull back while still in close contact with the enemy—a dangerous maneuver that could easily turn into a rout. Only Webster's rookies were available to try and stem the Confederate tide. The battle had become a race to see if the Confederates could push to the Dixville Crossroads before the reinforcements arrived to bolster McCook's men. The sun now also began to set, raising the stakes. If the Federals could only hold out a little while longer, darkness would save them.

Over on McCook's left, Colonel Starkweather had analyzed the ground behind him. A few hundred yards west of Starkweather Hill stood a ridge topped by a belt of woods and a stone wall that ran at right angles to the Benton Road. Half a mile beyond the stone wall was the Dixville Crossroads, and there were no more defensible positions between the wall and the intersection. The solution was obvious: Starkweather had to hold the ridge and the stone wall.[205]

Having decided where to retreat, Starkweather then turned to the problem of moving his cannon back. With so many horses out of action, it was up to the infantry to get these guns down the steep rear slope of Starkweather Hill and in position on the next ridge. While their comrades held off the Confederates, other men pulled the cannon back by hand as fast as they could. Only six of the twelve guns were withdrawn before a third Confederate charge swarmed over Starkweather Hill.[206]

The battered regiments of the 28th Brigade fell back under cover of their artillery. The three veteran units of this command fell back in good order, and Starkweather later commented that "all did so nobly and well" in holding back the Confederate attacks. Confusion reigned as the Federals regrouped behind the stone wall. Shattered units from the Open Knob battle congregated in the area, and survivors of the 21st Wisconsin milled around behind the wall. General Terrill was also present and received a mortal wound while trying to reorganize his men. General McCook appeared on horseback and helped Starkweather gather as many troops as possible to bolster the position.[207]

Starkweather's brigade fights in the cornfield. *Courtesy of the Library of Congress.*

Maney's and Stewart's Confederates crested Starkweather Hill about 4:30 p.m. and saw the stone wall position in front of them. These brigades were running out of time, men and energy. They had already taken two hills defended by Union infantry and artillery, and now faced a third. Most of the Confederate units had suffered over 40 percent casualties; several regiments had lost all of their field officers. For the third time that afternoon, these two Confederate brigades moved to the attack.[208]

Starkweather had his soldiers ready for this last charge. Packing the men six rows deep behind the wall, the Federals met the Confederates with a fusillade of bullets and cannon fire that "made sad havoc in their lines," according to the 21st Wisconsin's Sergeant Otto. Private Theodore Herrling of the 1st Wisconsin later described the battle from his perspective: "It was not generalship there, it was simply the fighting, staying qualities of the Union soldier." The Confederate infantry melted before this hail of lead and retreated to safety on the east slope of Starkweather Hill. With this final effort, the Confederates were played out on this flank; they had reached the High Water Mark of the Confederacy in the West.[209]

As the Confederates fell back, Starkweather's veterans charged forward to drive them from the field. The 1st Wisconsin's color-bearer, Sergeant John

Climax at the Dixville Crossroads

S. Durham, led the advance with an impetuosity that later earned him the Medal of Honor. A mêlée ensued atop Starkweather Hill, and a private of the 1st Wisconsin carried off a Confederate battle flag from Maney's brigade as a prize. The exhausted Confederates reeled back toward Open Knob in the face of this determined assault. As dusk fell, "the fire from the 79th and 24th held the enemy in check while the balance of the 1st Wisconsin took by hand every remaining gun and caisson from the field," reported Starkweather. Once the recovery work ended, Starkweather pulled his battered but victorious regiments back to the stone wall. The Confederates let them go unmolested.[210]

While Starkweather secured McCook's left flank, on the right Colonel George Webster's all-rookie 34th Brigade made its stand. Some of these men had taken part in halting Donelson's attacks earlier in the day, but most were seeing action for the first time at this point in the battle. Webster formed a line perpendicular to the Mackville Road along a ridge two hundred yards east of the intersection. John C. Russell's white house stood just to the

George Webster. *Perryville Battlefield State Historic Site.*

127

south. The 80[211] Indiana, 98th Ohio and 121st Ohio stood in front, while the 50th Ohio (whose colonel had deserted them) remained in reserve. Captain Samuel Harris's six-gun 19th Indiana Battery provided artillery support.[211]

The Confederates, for their part, "became so scattered in the pursuit… it [was] necessary to halt" and reform, according to General Cleburne. The Southerners pressed ahead again, with the brigades of Brown, Wood, Cleburne and Adams all trying to drive the Federals. Brown's brigade soon fell off the pace as General Brown suffered a wound and his men ran out of ammunition. Adams's men were distracted by III Corps artillery fire to their south and halted. Confederate artillery moved to Loomis Heights and started dueling with Harris's battery, while the infantry renewed its attack.[212]

Cleburne's and Wood's troops attacked the Federals head on, pushing to within yards of their position before being pinned down. Poor coordination blunted some of the Confederate power, but still they hit Webster's men hard. Colonel Webster tried to hold his rookies in line, but several units broke and ran. He went down with a mortal wound, and command of the 34th Brigade disintegrated. General Rousseau rallied some of Harris's and Lytle's men and personally led them to the ridge to help defend. Elements of the I Corps engineer detachment also went into battle as infantry. Rousseau moved up and down the line, oblivious to Confederate fire, waving his cap at the tip of his sword. His bravado had the desired effect upon the wavering Federal troops; the shaky line at the Russell House held together.[213]

General Cleburne later related the battle from his perspective:

> *I again advanced until within seventy-five yards of the position known as the white house, where a fresh line of the enemy were strongly posted, flanked by artillery. At this juncture I had no artillery and no supporting force upon my left. I sent Captain* [Charles H.] *Carlton, commanding a few sharpshooters, to watch my left. A large regiment posted in the valley to my right gave way, and most of them, in spite of my entreaties, fled to the rear, leaving my small brigade of not over 800 men in the center of the battle, unsupported on either flank. A furious cannonade between our own artillery, posted on the hill we first carried on the right of the Mackville road, and the enemy's artillery, posted on the right of the white house before mentioned, was carried on our own line. This, together with the fact that* [we] *were almost out of ammunition, prevented us from advancing farther.*

One of Cleburne's veterans,
Private John Rulle of the 2nd
Tennessee. *Perryville Battlefield
State Historic Site.*

John Rulle
2nd TN Inf. CS

As Cleburne's men held this dangerous position, the general suffered another wound that put him out of action temporarily. His brigade ground to a halt.[211]

Sam Wood's troops pushed even closer to the Federal line and managed to complete the destruction of Webster's force. Despite being wounded, General Wood led his men forward toward a fence defended by the 80th Indiana and the 121st Ohio. One of Wood's Alabamians later recalled,

> *We got to within 30 yards of the fence but our ranks were so badly thinned that we could not get to them. We stayed there for thirty minutes or more and there being no more troops to our right the Yankees came around our right and were getting behind us. Then Lt. Col [Robert F.] Crittenden ([Colonel Samuel] Adams being wounded) ordered us to fall back. So we got back to a depression, were halted and lay down, and while lieing*

[sic] *there firing our color bearer Neal Godwin said dinged if they aren't charging us and they were.*

The counterattack did not come from I Corps troops: Gooding's men had finally arrived on the field. [215]

Colonel Gooding, a Prussian army veteran, commanded a small brigade of three regiments totaling approximately 1,400 men. His troops had quick marched the two miles to the Dixville Crossroads and arrived about 5:15 p.m., shortly after Webster was killed. Gooding's guide described how they rounded a bend in the road and suddenly the battle came upon them:

There before me, within a few hundred yards, the battle of Perryville burst into view, and the roar of the artillery and the continuous rattle of the musketry first broke upon my ear. It was the finest spectacle I ever saw. It was wholly unexpected, and it fixed me with astonishment. It was like tearing away a curtain from the front of a great picture, or the sudden bursting of a thunder-cloud when the sky in front seems serene and clear. I

Michael Gooding. *Perryville Battlefield State Historic Site.*

had seen an unlooked-for storm at sea, with hardly a moment's notice, hurl
itself out of the clouds and lash the ocean into a foam of wild rage. But
here there was not the warning of an instant. At one bound my horse carried
me from stillness into the uproar of battle.

Colonel Gooding himself later explained, "On reaching the field I found the forces badly cut up and retreating (they then having fallen back nearly 1 mile) and were being hotly pressed by the enemy." His troops had appeared none too soon.[216]

General McCook met Gooding and explained the situation. Starkweather had secured the corps' left flank, but Rousseau's shaky line at the Russell House needed help to prevent its collapse. Without an immediate attack eastward into the Confederate advance, all might be lost. Gooding formed his three regiments (the veteran 22nd Indiana, the veteran 59th Illinois and the green 75th Illinois) in a "moment," according to a 22nd Indiana veteran. Placing the rookies in the center, with the 59th to the left and 22nd to the right, Gooding led his men forward. As the Indianans and Illinoisans advanced, Rousseau's line, "as soon as I had become engaged, retreated and fell back in confusion," reported Gooding.[217]

The sudden appearance of fresh Union troops on the attack staggered the Confederates. Some of Wood's men broke, forcing the entire Confederate line back toward Loomis Heights. Polk and Hardee now committed their last available brigade: St. John Liddell's Arkansas outfit, the same men who had defended Peters Hill that morning.[218]

Liddell deployed his veterans and moved forward about 5:45 p.m. The shadows were lengthening, and night closed in on the battlefield. His Arkansans got into a firefight with Gooding's Federals, forcing them back from their exposed position. Colonel Gooding also shifted the 22nd Indiana, his best regiment, to the left and the 59th Illinois to the right. The 75th Illinois stayed in the center. Gooding's men retreated to a small hillock just east and northeast of the Dixville Crossroads. Behind them, the battered remnants of McCook's corps had rallied and stood in support.[219]

By 6:30 p.m., the battle had wound down into a bloody stalemate as Gooding's Federals and Liddell's Confederates traded fire under the glow of a rising near-full moon. Still seeking a victory, at this moment General Polk rode forward to conduct a personal reconnaissance. In the fading light, his

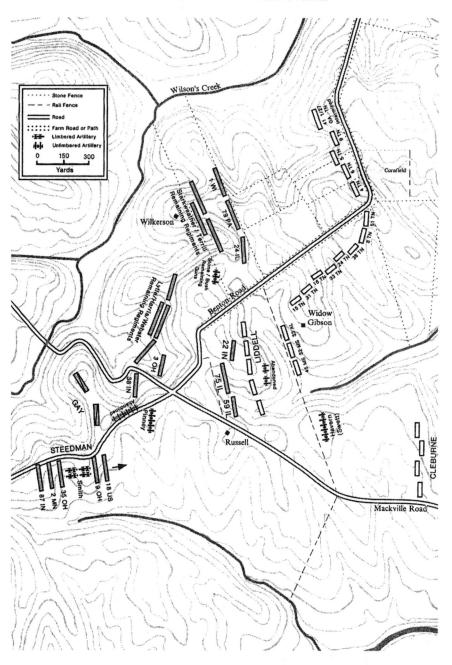

The Dixville Crossroads, 6:30 p.m. *Courtesy John P. Walsh Jr.*

dark-colored overcoat was indistinguishable from Union blue. The general had just joined Liddell when the cry came from the front, "Cease fire, you are firing upon friends." Once the shooting stopped, Polk rode through Liddell's soldiers to the next battle line and inquired, "What troops are these?"

The reply chilled him: "The 22nd Indiana, Lieutenant Colonel Squire Keith commanding." Polk, the second highest–ranking Confederate on the battlefield, was now among Union troops. As Polk ordered him to cease firing, Keith asked, "Who are you that gives this order?" General Polk again commanded him to cease firing or be court-martialed, which caused Keith to order his men to lower their weapons. The general rode along the 22nd's battle line, all the while feeling what he later described as "a thousand centipedes…traveling up and down my backbone." At the end, he spurred his horse back to Liddell's men and cried, "General, every mother's son of them are Yankees! Open fire!"[220]

Three volleys flamed in the darkness as Liddell's Arkansans opened up on the helpless Indianans. In less than ninety seconds, Lieutenant Colonel Keith was killed and 65 percent of his regiment lay dead or wounded— the highest percentage loss of any unit at Perryville. Several men were hit multiple times, and the 22nd's flag was lost in the confusion. After the brief flashes of gunfire, "I never before saw darkness come over the land [as] sudden as it did that time," remembered a survivor of the 22nd.[221]

General Liddell sensed an opportunity and renewed his advance. Gooding tried to rally his men for a defense, but fell wounded and was captured. The rest of his troops retired beyond the Dixville Crossroads, leaving the vital intersection at the mercy of the Confederate army.

Liddell felt the objective within his grasp and wanted to push forward and complete the victory. As he and Polk discussed the situation, they heard cheering to the south, announcing Steedman's arrival on the field. A shaken Polk turned to Liddell and declared, "I want no more night fighting." He ordered the Arkansans to hold in place. Confederate skirmishers stood at the Dixville Crossroads, maintaining a thin grip on the objective. The fighting was over on the northern end of the field.[222]

While McCook's I Corps was being pushed to the edge of destruction, on the Springfield Pike III Corps had become more active. Tennessean Colonel Samuel Powell commanded the small brigade left to guard the Confederate center near Bottom Hill. At 4:15 p.m., Powell sent his regiments west in a

James Steedman. *Perryville Battlefield State Historic Site.*

reconnaissance-in-force, which promptly ran into Sheridan's and Mitchell's rested troops. After a short but fierce battle, the Confederates fled east toward Perryville before superior numbers. Mitchell sent Colonel William Carlin's brigade in pursuit toward the city.[223]

Carlin paused on the outskirts of town to organize and deploy his artillery. His four cannon shelled downtown Perryville as Powell's men fled across the Chaplin River bridges. The gunners set several buildings on Main Street ablaze. After the bombardment stopped, Carlin sent the 21st and 38th Illinois Regiments into town. They secured the western part of Perryville by going house to house but did not have enough strength to cross the river and tangle with Powell's survivors, now reinforced by Preston Smith's veterans, the very last of Bragg's reserves. The Confederates occupied the buildings on the Chaplin's east side and traded fire with the Federals on the west side.[224]

Mitchell felt that a great opportunity was upon him and frantically appealed to Gilbert for reinforcements. The 9th Division commander wanted

Climax at the Dixville Crossroads

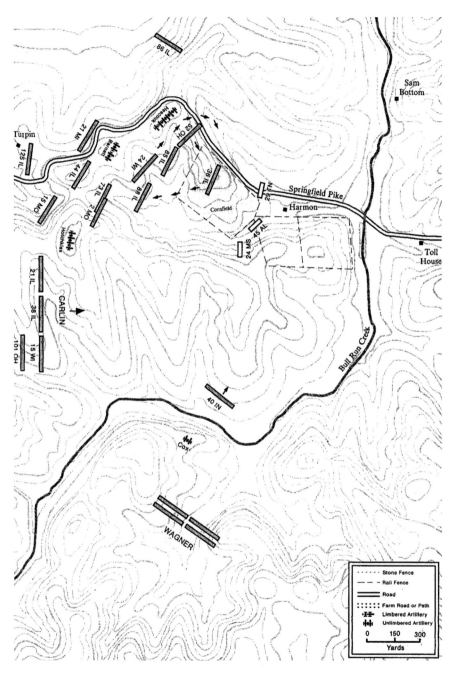

The Springfield Pike, 4:15 p.m. *Courtesy John P. Walsh Jr.*

to cross the river and get into Bragg's rear. Fearing a trap, Gilbert refused Mitchell's repeated requests. Several III Corps officers later felt that not pressing ahead was a serious error; Colonel Harlan lamented, "If Nelson had lived, and been in command of the middle [III] Corps, he would not have waited for orders, but would have regarded the actual fight going on…as a sufficient order that he should 'go in' and assist in defeating the enemy." But Bull Nelson was dead, and Gilbert was not in an aggressive mood. Darkness ended the fighting in Perryville, the first street combat of the Civil War.[225]

About 7:00 p.m., the Battle of Perryville drew to a close. For its size, the battle had been a very bloody affair. The Federals sustained 4,276 casualties while inflicting 3,401 losses on the Confederates. Most of those casualties came between the hours of 2:00 and 7:00 p.m. on October 8, 1862. In five hours of fighting, approximately 7,500 men had been killed, wounded or went missing, one of the worst per-hour casualty rates of the Civil War. "For the time engaged it was the severest and most desperately contested engagement within my knowledge," wrote General Bragg a few days after the battle.[226]

CHAPTER 11

RETREAT

That night both army commanders considered their options. Buell met with Gilbert, Thomas and McCook to discuss the situation. McCook's command had been badly bloodied, losing 25 percent of its strength in the afternoon's fighting. Rousseau's division had lost a brigade commander and 29 percent of its men, while the 10th Division (formerly under Jackson) had all of its senior leadership wiped out. These losses all reduced I Corps' effective fighting strength to barely more than a large division. III Corps had seen some fighting but remained fresh, while II Corps had hardly fired a shot all day. After weighing these reports, Buell issued orders for II and III Corps to attack at dawn the next day.[227]

Over on the Confederate side, General Bragg had watched the Battle of Perryville from his command post at the Samuel Crawford House on the city's north side. Although his men had won the day and mauled an entire Union corps, their situation was not very advantageous. Casualties had reduced Bragg's strength to thirteen thousand men, while leader losses further blunted his army's edge. The fighting in and around Perryville had finally convinced Bragg that Buell's entire army was present on the field. If the Confederates stayed and renewed the battle in the morning, they would likely be crushed by all three Federal corps. "Assured that the enemy had concentrated his three corps against us," Bragg later wrote, "and finding that our loss had already been quite heavy in the unequal contest against two, I gave the orders to fall back at daylight on Harrodsburg, and sent instructions to Major-General Smith to move his command to form a junction with me at that place." Tactically the Battle of Perryville may have been a success for the Confederates, but strategically it was a Union victory because Buell still held the better position. Bragg's plans had been dislocated by the battle, while Buell's campaign had not been altered in any way.[228]

As the high commands deliberated, an informal truce settled over the battlefield. McCook's Federals camped in the dark, but the Confederates lit campfires all along their lines. Both sides sent informal parties out to look after casualties. An Alabamian later recalled, "We were up with the wounded boys nearly all night. We went in squads of two, three or four without lights that night to where our dead comrades lay on the field and felt in their pockets to get their effects to send to their homes and find where they had been shot."[229]

Between 2:00 and 3:00 a.m. on October 9, the Confederates stole away from the Federals. Dawn found Bragg's army marching northeast to Harrodsburg, while Wheeler's cavalry stayed behind to protect the rear. Buell's dawn advance pushed into thin air and caught only a few stragglers. The Army of the Ohio spent the day at Perryville regrouping and preparing a pursuit for the next day.[230]

Thirty miles north of Perryville, outside Lawrenceburg, Kirby Smith's command hurried south to join Bragg at Harrodsburg. On the evening of October 8, the general received word that Sill was near Lawrenceburg and headed south, so he concentrated south of town to await developments. On the morning of October 9, Sill's leading units clashed with elements of Kirby Smith's army south of Lawrenceburg at Dry Ridge (also known as Dog Walk). After a sharp but inconclusive engagement that lasted all morning, the Confederates withdrew along the road south to Harrodsburg, twenty miles away.[231]

Bragg's army arrived in Harrodsburg on October 9 and spent the day reorganizing, paroling prisoners and resupplying. Kirby Smith's force arrived on October 10, and for the first time both Confederate armies were present and ready to fight the Federals on even terms. Bragg deployed his troops along ridges south and west of town to make a stand.[232]

On the morning of October 10, the Army of the Ohio set off in pursuit of the Confederates. To his credit, General Buell had not lost sight of his overall objective of pressuring Bragg's supply depot and line of communication to Tennessee. He personally took III Corps and I Corps northeast toward Harrodsburg to meet Sill and fight another battle, while Thomas led II

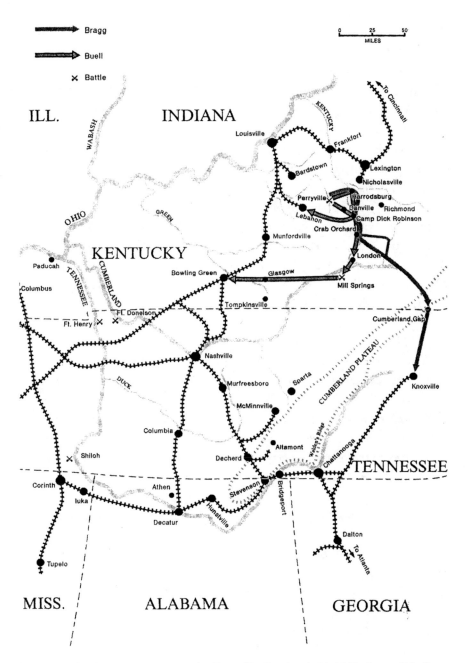

Union and Confederate movements after Perryville, October 9–24, 1862. *Courtesy John P. Walsh Jr.*

Corps east toward Danville and Camp Breckinridge in hopes of cutting Bragg off.[233]

Wheeler's cavalry skirmished with II Corps on the Danville Pike and quickly gave Bragg an understanding of Federal movements. Threatened in both his front and rear, Bragg initially favored giving battle at Harrodsburg. He soon thought better of it, and on October 11 withdrew his entire command fifteen miles southeast to Camp Breckinridge. There the Confederates decided to make a stand and try to salvage the campaign. Buell's army followed at a measured pace.[234]

As he sat among his supplies, Bragg must have reflected on how the Federals had outmaneuvered him over the past eleven days and wrecked his campaign. Gloom set in as he also recalled the failed recruiting efforts and how the bright prospects of the Kentucky Campaign had gone glimmering. On October 12, he sent an update to Richmond and gave vent to his frustration at the end of the message:

> *The campaign here was predicated on a belief and the most positive assurances that the people of this country would rise in mass to assert their independence. No people ever had so favorable an opportunity, but I am distressed to add there is little or no disposition to avail of it. Willing perhaps to accept their independence, they are neither disposed nor willing to risk their lives or their property in its achievement. With ample means to arm 20,000 men and a force with that to fully redeem the State we have not yet issued half the arms left us by casualties incident to the campaign.*

General Bragg had lost heart for the campaign and was looking for a way out.[235]

As it had throughout the Kentucky operation, the supply factor again disturbed Bragg's mind at Camp Breckinridge. First, the camp was found to have little more than four days' worth of rations for the entire Confederate force of forty-five thousand men. They could not withstand a siege or a major battle. Also, at this point the dry weather began to turn and autumn rains started. It would not be long before weather effectively closed the Wilderness Road over Cumberland Gap for the winter. Both of these factors forced Bragg to make an immediate decision whether to stay in Kentucky or retire southward.[236]

Retreat

On October 13, he decided to head back to Tennessee. That day, the Confederates pulled out of Camp Breckinridge and marched for Cumberland Gap and Knoxville. Anything they could not carry was destroyed. Buell's army methodically pursued, and Federal cavalry repeatedly clashed with Wheeler's horsemen. Terrain and bushwhackers also created problems for Bragg's soldiers, but by October 24 much of the army crossed through Cumberland Gap and back into Tennessee. The remainder followed within a few days, and by October 31 the Confederates had abandoned the Bluegrass State. Buell's troops pursued to just south of London and then broke off on October 19 and marched west toward the L&N Railroad.[237]

The decision to leave Kentucky was heartbreaking for Confederate Kentuckians. John Hunt Morgan remained with his cavalry at Lexington, and on October 17 he fought a small battle a mile outside of town in a futile effort to prevent Federal reoccupation of his hometown. Perhaps the saddest Kentuckians were John Breckinridge's Orphan Brigade soldiers, who were finally on their way to join Bragg in mid-October. They had not been anywhere near home since the previous February, and each day the anticipation grew as they marched north from Knoxville. When the Orphans camped on October 16, the mountains of Kentucky were in view. The next morning, the men formed up in full expectation of camping the following night in their home state. But just before the march began, a courier delivered orders to Breckinridge ordering them back to Knoxville. Bragg's decision to end the campaign made their move northward unnecessary.[238]

The Orphans returned to camp and spent the day there with the mountains still in view. "Thus the day wore on, and a painful day it was, too," commented one of the men. That evening in formation, the soldiers were quiet, "the silence of stern manhood bowed down by bitter disappointment," recalled Ed Thompson of the brigade. The next day, official word arrived of the Perryville defeat along with confirmation of the retreat. On October 19, the Orphans took one last look at home and turned south, not to return for the remainder of the war.[239]

General Buell's leisurely operations after Perryville had generated the ire of Washington, and by late October General Halleck was again looking for a new commander. Dissatisfaction with Buell had also grown within the Army of the Ohio's officer corps and threatened to spill into the open. On October 24, Buell was replaced by Major General William S. Rosecrans, a man who had recently won the Battle of Corinth. Before the year ended, Buell would face a court of inquiry (the Buell Commission) about the campaign, which issued mixed findings but preferred no charges. Rosecrans soon took the army into Tennessee and left Kentucky to the rear.[240]

Although the armies had moved on, the Battle of Perryville's effects lingered in Central Kentucky. Damage from the fighting had ruined farmers like John C. Russell and H.P. Bottom. Dead men also needed burying, a duty largely left up to local farmers. The sheer number of wounded on both sides flooded Perryville and the surrounding communities of Danville, Harrodsburg, Springfield and Lebanon. "Nearly every house was a hospital," reported Dr. A.N. Read of the U.S. Sanitary Commission in late October. "There had been almost no preparation for the care of the wounded at Perryville, and as a consequence the suffering from want of help of all kinds, as well as proper accommodations, food, medicines, and hospital stores, was excessive," he wrote.[241]

Perryville's Dr. Jefferson J. Polk lived downtown next to his office on Main Street. He was in the vortex of suffering virtually from the end of the battle:

> On the second morning after the battle of Perryville, or Chaplin Hills, I visited the battlefield. In passing out on the Springfield road, the fencing was all leveled to the ground—here and there a dead rebel. After proceeding about one mile, I came to a company of Union soldiers, who had collected ten or twelve of their dead comrades and were preparing to bury them... The first hospital I entered was Mr. Peters' house. Here were about two hundred wounded soldiers, lying side by side on beds of straw. Notwithstanding they were wounded in every possible way, there was not heard among them a groan or complaint. In the orchard close by a long trench had been dug, in which to bury the dead; about fifteen were lying in a row, ready for interment.
>
> I passed on northward, and saw on either hand dead men and dead horses, canteens, muskets, cartridge-boxes, broken ambulances, coats, hats, and shoes, scattered thick over the ground. I reached Mr. Russell's white house... Here was the center of the great battle. The house was dotted over with hundreds of marks of musket and cannon balls. All around lay dead bodies of the soldiers... In a skirt of woods close by were scattered

Retreat

hundreds of the dead of both armies...The ground was strewn with soiled and torn clothes, muskets, blankets, and the various accouterments of the dead soldiers. Trees not more than one foot in diameter contained from twenty to thirty musket-balls and buck-shot, put into them during the battle...I counted four hundred and ten dead men on a small spot of ground. My heart grew sick at the sight...I saw dead rebels piled up in pens like hogs. I reached my home, praying to God that I might never again be called upon to visit a battle-field...For months hundreds of the wounded died every week.

Dr. Polk tended forty wounded in a barn, while his home and office were crammed with sixty more men. The suffering lasted all winter and into the spring; Perryville's last hospital closed in March 1863.[242]

After October 1862, the dream of a Confederate Kentucky was dead forever; aside from cavalry raids, the Confederates never again penetrated the Bluegrass State. But for ten weeks in the summer of 1862, a Confederate Kentucky (with all the advantages it would convey) was tantalizingly within reach. Bragg's and Kirby Smith's victories brought the prospect within sight, but determined Federal leadership and movements ultimately defeated their often irresolute opponents. The Battle of Perryville, the state's largest and bloodiest, ensured that Kentucky would remain in the Union for the rest of the war.

Perryville also inaugurated a string of Union successes that led directly to the Confederate surrender at Durham Station, North Carolina, in 1865 at the end of the war. Although the Confederates would give a good account of themselves to the end, and faced several other opportunities for decisive success in the war, never again would their prospects be so bright in the Western Theater. The Battle of Perryville was the Southern apogee, the High Water Mark of the Confederacy in the West.

EPILOGUE

After the fall of 1862, the focus of the Western Theater shifted forever to Tennessee. Both armies received new names—the Army of the Ohio became the Army of the Cumberland, while Bragg's Army of the Mississippi turned into the Army of Tennessee. Below are some notes regarding the fate of various principal commanders in the 1862 Kentucky Campaign. Union and Confederate officers are listed together in alphabetical order.

JAMES PATTON ANDERSON reverted to brigade command after the Battle of Perryville and did not command a division again until late 1863. He surrendered at Durham Station, North Carolina, in April 1865.

BRAXTON BRAGG commanded the Army of Tennessee until December 1863, when he was relieved following a severe defeat outside Chattanooga, Tennessee. After a stint as military advisor to Jefferson Davis, Bragg took to the field in 1865 to help defend his home state. He surrendered at Durham Station in April 1865.

SIMON BOLIVAR BUCKNER commanded a corps in 1863 and later served as chief of staff to Kirby Smith in the Trans-Mississippi Theater. After the war, he became governor of Kentucky. His son later served in the U.S. Army and was killed in action commanding the Tenth Army during the Battle of Okinawa in 1945.

DON CARLOS BUELL never held a field command after October 1862. Offered a post in 1864 under Major General William T. Sherman, he refused to serve under a junior officer. Buell resigned from the U.S. Army in June 1864.

WILLIAM P. CARLIN commanded a brigade and later a division with distinction in Tennessee, Georgia and the Carolinas. After the war, he served on the frontier with the U.S. Army.

BENJAMIN F. CHEATHAM commanded his division throughout 1863 and rose to corps command in 1864 and 1865. He surrendered at Durham Station in 1865.

PATRICK R. CLEBURNE fought his last battle as a brigade commander at Perryville. Promoted to full-time division command, he became the best officer at that level in the Army of Tennessee. He was killed in action at the Battle of Franklin, Tennessee, on November 30, 1864.

THOMAS L. CRITTENDEN led his corps until October 1863, when he was removed for fleeing from the Battle of Chickamauga, Georgia, in the face of a massive Confederate breakthrough. He later commanded a division in Virginia in 1864 and returned to Louisville after the war.

JEFFERSON C. DAVIS was never tried for the murder of Bull Nelson. After a short stay in prison, he was released in time to command a division under McCook at the Battle of Stones River, Tennessee, at the end of 1862. He commanded a division in the Army of the Cumberland until the fall of Atlanta in September 1864 and later XIV Corps in the Carolinas Campaign.

DANIEL DONELSON commanded his brigade for the rest of 1862 and then went on medical leave. He died of natural causes in April 1863.

CHARLES C. GILBERT was never confirmed by Congress as a major general and reverted to his previous rank of captain. He finished the war in a series of minor quartermaster posts.

MICHAEL GOODING received a parole after his capture and commanded the 22nd Indiana until leaving the army in 1864.

WILLIAM J. HARDEE commanded a corps in the Army of Tennessee in 1863 and 1864, and briefly the army itself after Bragg's relief. After surrendering Savannah to Sherman's forces in December 1864, Hardee fought in the Carolinas Campaign, where his only son was killed in March 1865. General Hardee surrendered at Durham Station.

LEONARD HARRIS fought his last battle at Perryville. He resigned his commission in December 1862.

THOMAS JONES reverted to regimental command after Perryville. He resigned from the Confederate army in early 1863 and returned to civilian life in Mississippi.

ST. JOHN R. LIDDELL commanded his brigade and later a division in the Army of Tennessee until the end of 1863. He subsequently commanded coastal defenses in Mississippi and Alabama. General Liddell surrendered at Fort Blakely, Alabama, on April 9, 1865.

WILLIAM H. LYTLE recovered from his wound and returned to field command. He was killed in action at the Battle of Chickamauga on September 20, 1863.

GEORGE E. MANEY commanded his brigade and later a division in all the subsequent campaigns of the Army of Tennessee until suffering a serious wound at the Battle of Jonesboro, Georgia, in 1864. He was paroled in North Carolina in 1865.

ALEXANDER McCOOK commanded his corps until October 1863, when he was removed for fleeing the Battle of Chickamauga with Crittenden. McCook later commanded troops in Washington, D.C. In 1896, General McCook was the U.S. representative to the coronation of Czar Nicholas II in Russia.

DANIEL McCOOK stayed in brigade command after the Battle of Perryville. He was mortally wounded on June 27, 1864, at the Battle of Kennesaw Mountain in Georgia.

GEORGE W. MORGAN later commanded a division in the Vicksburg Campaign. Stung by criticism for abandoning Cumberland Gap, he quarreled with Halleck and resigned from the U.S. Army in June 1863.

JOHN HUNT MORGAN commanded several brilliant cavalry operations in 1862 and 1863, including a foray into Indiana and Ohio. He was killed by Federal raiders in Greeneville, Tennessee, on September 4, 1864.

LEONIDAS POLK held a succession of senior commands in the Western Theater and the Army of Tennessee. He was killed in action at Pine Mountain, Georgia, on June 14, 1864.

LOVELL H. ROUSSEAU commanded his division until the summer of 1863, when ill health forced him to take a rear-area command. After the war, he received Alaska from the Russians on behalf of the United States.

JOHN SAVAGE commanded the 16th Tennessee until January 1863, when he resigned from the Confederate Army.

PHILIP H. SHERIDAN stayed in division command throughout 1863 and rose to corps and army command in 1864 and 1865 in Virginia. He played a decisive role in forcing Robert E. Lee's Army of Northern

Virginia to surrender in April 1865. After the war, he fought on the frontier and commanded the United States Army from 1883 to 1888.

JOSHUA SILL reverted to brigade command in Sheridan's division as part of a reorganization in November 1862. He was killed in action at the Battle of Stones River, Tennessee, on December 31, 1862. Sheridan later named Fort Sill, Oklahoma, in his honor.

EDMUND KIRBY SMITH commanded all Confederate forces west of the Mississippi River from 1863 to 1865. After the fall of Vicksburg, this area became a semiautonomous fiefdom known as "Kirby Smithdom." On May 26, 1865, he surrendered the last of the Confederacy's land forces in North America.

JOHN C. STARKWEATHER commanded his brigade with distinction throughout 1863 until ill health forced him from active service. He left the U.S. Army in 1865 and returned to Wisconsin.

CARTER L. STEVENSON was transferred to Mississippi at the end of 1862, where he surrendered at Vicksburg. After being exchanged, he commanded a division in the Army of Tennessee during all its battles in 1864 and 1865. He surrendered at Durham Station.

ALEXANDER P. STEWART later commanded a division and a corps in the Army of Tennessee. He surrendered at Durham Station in 1865.

GEORGE H. THOMAS became a corps commander in the Army of the Cumberland after Perryville, earning lasting fame as "The Rock of Chickamauga" for his stand at that battle in September 1863. He commanded the Army of the Cumberland from October 1863 until the end of the war, leading it to a signal victory at Nashville, Tennessee, in December 1864. Thomas died in 1870, still despised by his Virginia relatives for remaining with the Union.

JOHN A. WHARTON commanded cavalry in Tennessee and Louisiana. He was killed during an argument with a fellow officer on April 6, 1865.

JOSEPH WHEELER led the Army of Tennessee's cavalry for the remainder of the war, surrendering at Durham Station in 1865. In 1898, he rejoined the U.S. Army and commanded cavalry during the Santiago Campaign and the Battle of San Juan Hill in Cuba.

JOHN T. WILDER was exchanged and commanded the famed Lightning Brigade of mounted infantry at the Battle of Chickamauga. He resigned from the U.S. Army in 1864 because of frail health. After the war, Wilder became mayor of Chattanooga, Tennessee.

THE OPPOSING FORCES AT PERRYVILLE

(k=killed; w=wounded; mw=mortally wounded; wc=wounded and captured)

Army of the Ohio
Maj. Gen. Don Carlos Buell
Maj. Gen. George H. Thomas (second in command)
4th U.S. Cavalry (escort)

I Army Corps
Maj. Gen. Alexander McCook

3rd Division
Brig. Gen. Lovell H. Rousseau

9th Brigade
Col. Leonard A. Harris
38th Indiana
2nd Ohio
33rd Ohio
94th Ohio
10th Wisconsin
5th Battery Indiana Light Artillery

Appendix I

17th Brigade
Col. William H. Lytle (wc)
Col. Curran Pope
42nd Indiana
88th Indiana
15th Kentucky
3rd Ohio
10th Ohio
Battery A, 1st Michigan Light Artillery

28th Brigade
Col. John C. Starkweather
24th Illinois
79th Pennsylvania
1st Wisconsin
21st Wisconsin
4th Battery Indiana Light Artillery
Battery A, 1st Kentucky Light Artillery

10th Division
Brig. Gen. James S. Jackson (k)
Brig. Gen. William R. Terrill (mw)
Colonel Albert S. Hall

33rd Brigade
Brig. Gen. William R. Terrill (mw)
Colonel Albert S. Hall
80th Illinois
123rd Illinois
Garrard's Detachment (elements 7th Kentucky, 32nd Kentucky and 3rd
Tennessee U.S.)
105th Ohio
Parsons' Independent Battery Light Artillery

34th Brigade
Col. George Webster (mw)

The Opposing Forces at Perryville

80th Indiana
50th Ohio
98th Ohio
121st Ohio
19th Battery Indiana Light Artillery

Unattached
1st Michigan Engineers and Mechanics (detachment)

II Army Corps
Maj. Gen. Thomas L. Crittenden

4th Division
Brig. Gen. William Sooy Smith

10th Brigade
Col. William Grose
36th Indiana
84th Illinois
23rd Kentucky
6th Ohio
24th Ohio
Battery H, 4th U.S. Artillery
Battery M, 4th U.S. Artillery

19th Brigade
Col. William B. Hazen
110th Illinois
9th Indiana
6th Kentucky
27th Kentucky
41st Ohio
Battery F, 1st Ohio Light Artillery

22nd Brigade
Brig. Gen. Charles Cruft

31st Indiana
1st Kentucky
2nd Kentucky
20th Kentucky
90th Ohio
Battery B, 1st Ohio Light Artillery

5th Division
Brig. Gen. Horatio P. Van Cleve

11th Brigade
Col. Samuel Beatty
79th Indiana
9th Kentucky
13th Kentucky
19th Ohio
59th Ohio
7th Battery Indiana Light Artillery

14th Brigade
Col. Pierce Hawkins
14th Indiana
86th Indiana
11th Kentucky
26th Kentucky
13th Ohio
Battery B, Pennsylvania Light Artillery

23rd Brigade
Col. Stanley Matthews
8th Kentucky
21st Kentucky
35th Indiana
51st Ohio
99th Ohio
3rd Battery Wisconsin Light Artillery

The Opposing Forces at Perryville

6th Division
Brig. Gen. Thomas J. Wood

15th Brigade
Brig. Gen. Milo S. Hascall
26th Ohio
3rd Kentucky
17th Indiana
58th Indiana
100th Illinois
8th Battery Indiana Light Artillery

20th Brigade
Col. Charles G. Harker
64th Ohio
65th Ohio
13th Michigan
51st Indiana
73rd Indiana
6th Battery Ohio Light Artillery

21st Brigade
Col. George D. Wagner
15th Indiana
40th Indiana
57th Indiana
97th Ohio
24th Kentucky
10th Battery Indiana Light Artillery

Unattached
1st Michigan Engineers and Mechanics (detachment)
1st Ohio Cavalry (detachment)
3rd Ohio Cavalry (detachment)

Appendix I

III Army Corps
Acting Maj. Gen. Charles C. Gilbert

1st Division
Brig. Gen. Albin Schoepf

1st Brigade
Col. Moses B. Walker
17th Ohio
31st Ohio
38th Ohio
12th Kentucky
82nd Indiana
Battery D, 1st Michigan Light Artillery

2nd Brigade
Brig. Gen. Speed Fry
14th Ohio
4th Kentucky
10th Kentucky
10th Indiana
74th Indiana
Battery C, 1st Ohio Light Artillery

3rd Brigade
Brig. Gen. James B. Steedman
18th U.S.
9th Ohio
2nd Minnesota
87th Indiana
35th Ohio
Battery I, 4th U.S. Artillery

9th Division
Brig. Gen. Robert B. Mitchell

The Opposing Forces at Perryville

30th Brigade
Col. Michael Gooding (wc)
Lt. Col. John Bennett
22nd Indiana
59th Illinois
74th Illinois (detached guarding trains; not engaged)
75th Illinois
5th Battery Wisconsin Light Artillery

31st Brigade
Col. William P. Carlin
15th Wisconsin
101st Ohio
21st Illinois
38th Illinois
2nd Minnesota Battery

32nd Brigade
Col. William W. Caldwell
8th Kansas
81st Indiana
35th Illinois
25th Illinois
8th Battery Wisconsin Light Artillery

11th Division
Brig. Gen. Philip H. Sheridan

35th Brigade
Lt. Col. Bernard Laiboldt
2nd Missouri
15th Missouri
44th Illinois
73rd Illinois

36th Brigade

Col. Daniel McCook
52nd Ohio
85th Illinois
86th Illinois
125th Illinois

37th Brigade

Col. Nicholas Greusel
24th Wisconsin
21st Michigan
36th Illinois
88th Illinois

11th Division Artillery

Battery I, 2nd Illinois Light Artillery
Battery G, 1st Missouri Light Artillery

2nd Cavalry Brigade

Col. Edward M. McCook
1st Kentucky Cavalry
2nd Kentucky Cavalry
3rd Kentucky Cavalry
7th Pennsylvania Cavalry

3rd Cavalry Brigade

Acting Brig. Gen. Ebenezer Gay
2nd Michigan Cavalry
9th Kentucky Cavalry
9th Pennsylvania Cavalry

Army of the Mississippi

Gen. Braxton Bragg

Right Wing

Maj. Gen. Leonidas Polk

The Opposing Forces at Perryville

1st Division
Maj. Gen. Benjamin F. Cheatham

1st Brigade
Brig. Gen. Daniel S. Donelson
8th Tennessee
15th Tennessee
16th Tennessee
38th Tennessee
51st Tennessee
Carnes's Tennessee Battery

2nd Brigade
Brig. Gen. Alexander P. Stewart
4th Tennessee
5th Tennessee
24th Tennessee
31st Tennessee
33rd Tennessee
Stanford's Mississippi Battery

3rd Brigade
Brig. Gen. George E. Maney
41st Georgia
1st Tennessee
6th Tennessee
9th Tennessee
27th Tennessee
Turner's Mississippi Battery

4th Brigade
Col. Preston Smith
12th Tennessee
13th Tennessee
47th Tennessee
154th Tennessee Senior

9th Texas
Scott's Tennessee Battery

Wharton's Cavalry Brigade
Col. John A. Wharton
Davis's Tennessee Cavalry Battalion
2nd Georgia Battalion
8th Texas Cavalry
4th Tennessee Cavalry
1st Kentucky Cavalry (detachment)

Left Wing
Maj. Gen. William J. Hardee

1st Division
Brig. Gen. James Patton Anderson

1st Brigade
Brig. Gen. John C. Brown (w)
1st Florida
3rd Florida
41st Mississippi
Battery A, 14th Georgia Artillery

2nd Brigade
Brig. Gen. Daniel W. Adams
13th Louisiana
16th Louisiana
20th Louisiana
25th Louisiana
14th Battalion Louisiana Sharpshooters
5th Company, Washington Artillery

3rd Brigade
Col. Samuel Powell
24th Mississippi

29th Tennessee
1st Arkansas
45th Alabama
Barret's Missouri Battery

4th Brigade
Col. Thomas M. Jones
27th Mississippi
30th Mississippi
34th Mississippi
Lumsden's Alabama Battery

2nd Division
Maj. Gen. Simon B. Buckner

1st Brigade
Brig. Gen. St. John R. Liddell
2nd Arkansas
5th Arkansas
6th Arkansas
7th Arkansas
8th Arkansas
Swett's Mississippi Battery

2nd Brigade
Brig. Gen. Patrick R. Cleburne (w)
Col. Benjamin Hill
13th/15th Arkansas
2nd Tennessee
35th Tennessee
48th Tennessee
Calvert's Arkansas Battery

3rd Brigade
Brig. Gen. Bushrod R. Johnson
5th Confederate

17th Tennessee
23rd Tennessee
25th Tennessee
37th Tennessee
44th Tennessee
Darden's Mississippi Battery

4th Brigade
Brig. Gen. Sterling A.M. Wood (w)
3rd Georgia Cavalry (Detachment)
3rd Confederate
15th Mississippi Sharpshooters Battalion
45th Mississippi
16th Alabama
33rd Alabama
Semple's Alabama Battery

Wheeler's Cavalry Brigade
Col. Joseph Wheeler
1st Alabama Cavalry
3rd Alabama Cavalry
6th Confederate Cavalry
8th Confederate Cavalry
2nd Georgia Cavalry
Smith's Georgia Cavalry Legion
1st Kentucky Cavalry (detachment)
6th Kentucky Cavalry
9th Tennessee Cavalry
12th Tennessee Cavalry Battalion
Hanley's Section, Calvert's Arkansas Battery

THE BUELL PETITION

During the campaign, several of the officers from Charles Gilbert's III Corps met behind closed doors and decided to petition President Lincoln for Buell's removal from army command. The Buell Commission addressed the issue of dissatisfaction among the Army of the Ohio's officers as part of its investigation, and details about that conference and its purposes came to light. Yet some confusion about the petition and its timing persists to this day.

Federal officers did meet and did sign an appeal to President Lincoln, but it was never sent. The meeting took place near Lebanon, Kentucky, in a building (variously described as a house or schoolhouse) along the Rolling Fork River. Brigadier General Albin Schoepf, an anti-Buell officer and division commander in Gilbert's corps, convened it. Brigadier Generals James B. Steedman and Speed Fry presided and some twenty-one officers attended, representing virtually all of the line commanders in the III Corps. However, some question exists as to when that conference actually occurred.

Recent scholars of the Perryville Campaign have placed the meeting on October 7, 1862, the eve of the Battle of Perryville. This interpretation has most recently appeared in the excellent books by Kenneth Noe about the battle and Larry J. Daniel on the Army of the Cumberland. Both of them state categorically that the conference occurred on the eve of battle in Schoepf's 1st Division headquarters. The 1st Division was a part of III Corps and that night stood a few miles west of Perryville and in proximity to the enemy. Such a meeting is an extraordinary event on the eve of battle, and deserves comment. Yet no such gathering occurred on the night of October 7.

The conference of III Corps officers did take place, but not until weeks after the battle and after Buell and Bragg broke contact. A close reading of Buell Commission testimony gives a strong indication that the meeting occurred toward the end of the campaign, when the III Corps was moving west through Central Kentucky toward Bowling Green.

Major General Alexander McCook was an early witness before the Buell Commission. He was asked about the meeting by both Generals Schoepf and Buell, and he provided the following information (emphasis added):

> *General SCHOEPF. What do you know of the dissatisfaction of the officers and men and the petition sent with respect to the removal of General Buell* after *the battle of Perryville?*
>
> *I was informed while* on the march from Danville to Lebanon *that there was such a paper in existence in General Gilbert's corps. Who was the originator of it I do not know. I never saw the paper. The first development of this feeling of dissatisfaction I discovered on the march from Nashville to Louisville. They complained of being marched to death and of being half fed. Another cause of this dissatisfaction was that General Buell was always very much engaged in his quarters and did not go around among his soldiers much. I have frequently felt that had he visited his camps more, reviewed his troops more, and shown himself more to his soldiers a different state of feeling would have existed. I always had confidence in General Buell as a general, and, thank God, I have yet.*
>
> *By General BUELL:*
>
> *Question. Do you know the names of the signers of the paper referred to?*
> *I had a conversation with one of them outside the door here a few moments ago. I asked him about it, as to whether he ever heard of such a meeting of officers in the army wishing to depose General Buell and put General Thomas in command, and in this conversation with General Steedman he said he had signed a paper and had presided at a meeting of officers requesting the President to remove General Buell. I think General Steedman has confidence in General Buell, but was influenced by the junior officers and men in his command.*
>
> *Question. Where was that meeting held?*

*I did not know, but somewhere on the Rolling Fork. I knew nothing
for certain, but believe it was so.* It was subsequent to the battle
of Perryville; *but their feeling was more particularly directed against
General Gilbert.*

Question. Did the paper state any reason?
*I never saw the paper. It was merely mentioned on the way down, but it
was by officers I had no control over. I knew of no other officers that signed
it. General Steedman said it was a respectful petition to the President of the
United States. He thought it the most direct road to the President.*

Although Alexander McCook was not present at the conference, he clearly
was aware of what occurred and when. Schoepf's question also specifically
asked about the period *after* the Battle of Perryville.[243]

James B. Steedman, one of Schoepf's brigade commanders and one of
the meeting's presiding officers, gave many details about the conference to
the Commission:

*Question. Were these charges of disloyalty made against General Buell by
officers in high rank?*
*I have heard officers of the rank of brigadier-general, colonels, and
lieutenant-colonels charge General Buell with disloyalty.*

*Question. Did you ever hear these officers make such charges in the presence
or hearing of their inferiors in rank?*
I have.

*Question. State the names of the officers making these charges and in whose
presence they were made.*
I decline to do that unless positively required so to do.

*Question. You are not required to give any testimony which would
implicate yourself.*
*The reason I decline was under the rule which shields the court, the jury,
and the witnesses. If I am required to state I will, with the declaration in
advance that I have heard a member of the court say so.*

The court decided that the question be put.

I have heard General Schoepf, in my presence, declare General Buell's disloyalty; I have heard the colonel of the Fourteenth Ohio, George P. Este, in the presence of several officers of his regiment, doubt the loyalty of General Buell; I have heard the lieutenant-colonel commanding (I think) the Eighth Kansas Regiment charge General Buell with disloyalty in the presence of superiors. There were quite a number of officers present, but I think no inferiors. I am unable to recollect all the officers by name. I frequently heard officers express doubts of General Buell's loyalty.

By General DANA:
Question. Did you ever hear these declarations made by officers of any rank in the presence or hearing of enlisted men?
No, sir; I do not think I did. I have no recollection of having so heard.

Question. Who were the superior officers before whom the lieutenant-colonel of the Eighth Kansas Volunteers made allegations against the commanding general as to his loyalty?
[General Steedman declined to answer the question unless so ordered by the commission.]

The PRESIDENT. Was it at a public meeting?
It was a meeting held in the camp at Rolling Fork, 6 or 7 miles from Lebanon, Ky., at the house of a citizen, and it was generally understood among the officers of the several commands that they were to assemble at that time and place. It was held with closed doors, to exclude its proceedings from the enlisted men of the army.

The PRESIDENT. It is the opinion of the court that, without criminating yourself, you can answer the question.
I do not feel that it would be incriminating myself to state all I know about it. I did not think there was anything criminal in the meeting at the time nor do I now. We were present for the purpose of conferring with each other as to the condition of the army, and interchange of opinions as to the feeling toward the commander-in-chief of the Army of the Ohio; and after it assembled there was a great deal of discussion as to the best manner

of expressing our opinions in relation to General Buell. The result was a dispatch to the President was agreed upon, asking him to relieve General Buell from the command of the army, for the reason that, in the opinion of the signers, he had lost its confidence. That dispatch was signed by all the officers who were present. It was during the discussion upon the several propositions made before the meeting that that officer, in the course of his remarks, expressed his doubt as to the loyalty of General Buell. I do not remember his name, but my understanding was that he was the lieutenant-colonel commanding the Eighth Kansas Regiment. I never saw him before and have never seen him since. I think all the colonels commanding regiments in the First Division were present at that meeting. There may have been one or two absent, but my recollection is that they were all there. The brigade commanders of the First Division were all there, and one division commander, General Fry.[244] *There were a number of colonels from either General Mitchell's or General Sheridan's division, I am not positive which, but the officers commanding regiments in Col. Daniel McCook's brigade were present. Colonel Post, commanding a brigade, was present; I think he was of General Mitchell's division. The last time I saw that dispatch to the President it was in the hands of Col. John M. Harlan, commanding the Second Brigade in the First Division, and my recollection now is that there were either twenty-one or thirty-one, I am not positive which, commanders of regiments' names to it. I am positive there were twenty-one.*

Steedman clearly establishes the location of the meeting as near Lebanon, with some details as to participants and their answers. He also clearly states that Colonel John M. Harlan of the 10th Kentucky (and future U.S. Supreme Court justice) was given charge of the signed petition for transmission to Washington.[245]

Speed Fry, another one of Schoepf's brigadiers at Perryville and the meeting's other facilitator, also described the conference to the commission (emphasis added):

Question. Do you know of any petition to remove General Buell from the command of the Army of the Ohio either before or after the battle *of Perryville?*
I know of only one and that was never presented.

Question. What was this petition based upon?
Simply upon the idea that those signing it did not believe General Buell was commanding the army in such a manner as to secure success for our arms.

Question. Did it make any specific charges against General Buell?
None that I recollect except that.

Question. About how many colonels of regiments signed this petition?
I did not count the number. Eight or ten, I suppose; perhaps more; not less, I am satisfied.

Question. Did you consider at the time that this petition was right and well founded?
I thought it was well founded at the time.

This question being objected to by the judge-advocate, the court was cleared.

Question. Do you know the names of any officers of the rank of colonel or above that rank who signed this petition?
Yes, sir.

Question. Will you state those names?
General James B. Steedman, Third Brigade of the First Division; Col. J.M. Harlan, commanding Second Brigade of the First Division; Colonel George, commanding Second Minnesota Regiment; Col. J.M. Connell, commanding Seventeenth Ohio; Col. M.B. Walker, commanding First Brigade, First Division; Col. John T. Croxton, commanding Fourth Kentucky; Maj. D. Ward, of the Seventeenth Ohio; Lieut. Col. F.W. Lister, of the Thirty-first Ohio, and several others whose names I cannot now call to mind.

Question. Did you sign this petition?
I decline to answer that question, sir.

Fry corroborates much of Steedman's account and places many of the same people at the meeting. He also states that only one meeting occurred.[246]

The Buell Petition

On the eve of the Battle of Perryville, the III Corps stood about three miles west of Perryville. Lebanon is located ten miles to the southwest of Perryville, and the meeting took place a farther six to seven miles beyond that town. It is unlikely that any senior officer would leave his troops when in proximity to the enemy and ride sixteen miles away to have a private conference. Less plausible is that twenty-one different commanders would all make the same choice the night before a major battle. The III Corps did pass from Danville through the Lebanon area late in October 1862, just before Buell was relieved on October 24; it is believable that all these III Corps officers met in a building close to the corps' camp during that period.

The last, and definitive, word on the conference comes from Colonel Harlan himself, who wrote the following detailed account after the war. Neither Noe nor Daniel reviewed this letter, and as far as can be ascertained this account has not been widely available before now. Harlan's regiment, the 10th Kentucky, was raised from the area of Springfield, Lebanon and Danville.

Our army then returned [from pursuing Bragg] *and went into camp, our Division making their camp on the Rolling Fork of Salt River about 10 miles from Lebanon, Kentucky. The next day after we went into camp,* [a] *message came that a meeting of the field officers of our corps, Gilbert's, would be held at the little schoolhouse up the creek, and that my presence there was desired. The object of the meeting was not stated, but in view of the feeling that Bragg has been permitted to escape with all his troops, I suspected that the proposed meeting had some mischievous or dangerous purpose in contemplation. But I determined to know what was going on, feeling that whatever was said or done at the meeting, I knew my duty and could take care of myself.*

So I went at the appropriate time, and found about twenty officers there... Soon the talking commenced, all that was said for some time being directed against Gilbert, our corps commander. He was pronounced as incompetent for his position and it was said that his removal was vital to the army. It was suggested that a telegram on the subject should be sent directly and at once to President Lincoln. Finally, a Lieutenant Colonel or Major of an Illinois Regiment—whose name, I think, was McClellan or McLellan [Lieutenant Colonel James McClelland of the 25th Illinois

Infantry]—*rose and said with impassioned voice: "Mr. Chairman, I rise to say that, in my opinion, we are a pack of cowards." What do you mean?" said Col. Fry* [sic] *He replied: "I mean that we have spent all this evening talking about Gen. Gilbert, when our real objection is to Buell our commander. In my opinion, Buell is a traitor, is untrue to the army and untrue to the country."*

When he sat down, I arose, feeling that…I could not pass in silence what the Illinois officer had said, without expressing my own views. So I said, in substance: "Mr. Chairman, I do not concur in what has been said about Gen. Buell. He no doubt has made mistakes, and may have some views that I do not share. But I do not believe that he is untrue to the army or that he purposely or treacherously allowed Bragg's army to escape. Nor will I sign any telegram to the President which would question Buell's integrity or his fidelity to his troops." "What sort of a telegram," broke in the Illinois officer, "will you sign? Put down on paper what you are willing to say."

Thereupon I sat down at the table, and wrote a telegram such as I would consent to be sent to the President. It ran about in this wise: "Gen. Buell having lost the confidence of the Army of the Ohio, we think that the public interests would be subserved by a change of commanders." "That," the Illinois officer said, "is satisfactory." We all (including Gen. Steedman and Gen. Fry) signed it and, much to my surprise, the telegram was committed to me to be sent to Washington.

The next day I started for Lebanon, where a telegraph office was located, intending to send the proposed telegram. On my way, it occurred to me that the telegram would go through Buell's headquarters, and that all of those who had signed it would get into trouble. But I made up my mind to do what my brother officers desired, and which I had agreed to do. Luckily for us, upon my arrival at Lebanon, the Louisville papers of that day announced that by order of the President, Buell had been superseded by Gen. [William S.] Rosecrans in command of the army…I took the responsibility of withholding the telegram.[247]

Harlan's account corroborates the Buell Commission testimony in all important details, and places the timeframe clearly at the end of October, just before Buell's relief on October 24. The actual date of the meeting was on or about October 23. He also gives the best evidence why the petition never reached Washington.

The III Corps officers clearly were displeased with their army commander, but they waited until the campaign's end to try and make their feelings known. The eve-of-battle meeting is a great legend, but in the face of this evidence must remain merely a story.

Notes

Chapter 1

1. Noe, *Perryville*, 31.
2. Ibid., 27–28; see also Parks, *Kirby Smith*, 1–199.
3. Noe, *Perryville*, 15–17; see also McWhiney, *Braxton Bragg*, 1–173. McWhiney states that Bragg was born at home, while Noe claims that Bragg was born while his mother was in jail. Bragg's brother Thomas was governor of North Carolina from 1855 to 1859 and one of the state's U.S. senators in 1861 when the state seceded. He later served as Confederate attorney general in 1861 and 1862.
4. Noe, *Perryville*, 28–32; Parks, *Kirby Smith*, 198; see also Daniel, *Days of Glory*.
5. Harrison, *Civil War in Kentucky*, 1–13; the Lincoln quote comes from a letter to O.H. Browning, September 22, 1861, typescript in the files of Perryville Battlefield State Historic Site (hereafter cited as PBSHS).
6. Harrison, *Civil War in Kentucky*, 23–32; see also Daniel, *Days of Glory*, 33–73.
7. Noe, *Perryville*, 19–20; a fine account of the battle can be found in Catton, *Grant Moves South*.
8. Daniel, *Days of Glory*, 75–106.
9. Ibid., 91–106.
10. Noe, *Perryville*, 23–31. Bragg's rail movement was the first major strategic use of railways in the Civil War.
11. Parks, *Kirby Smith*, 200–02; for a slightly different account see Noe, *Perryville*, 23–31.

12. This paragraph is constructed primarily using Parks, *Kirby Smith*, 201–3; the "siren song" quote comes from Noe, *Perryville*, 31; the John Hunt Morgan dispatch is from *War of the Rebellion*, series I, vol. 16, part 2, 733–34.
13. War of the Rebellion, vol. 16, part 2, 748–49.

Chapter 2

14. Parks, *Kirby Smith*, 204–6; *War of the Rebellion*, vol. 16, part 1, 992.
15. For an explanation of Kirby Smith's army and its composition, see Hafendorfer, *Battle of Richmond Kentucky*, 11–29, 393–94.
16. Ibid., 17–20.
17. Ibid., 47–55; Noe, *Perryville*, 37–39.
18. Hafendorfer, *Battle of Richmond Kentucky*, 31–41. General Boyle was from Danville, Kentucky. Danville is the county seat of Boyle County, which was created in 1842 and named for his father. Perryville is in the western end of Boyle County.
19. Ibid.; see also Richardson, *Cassius Marcellus Clay*, 46, 86–87. Clay's estate, Whitehall, is now a Kentucky State Historic Site.
20. Daniel, *Days of Glory*, 5–6, 79–84, 116–17.
21. Hafendorfer, *Battle of Richmond Kentucky*, 63–71; Richardson, *Cassius Marcellus Clay*, 87–88.
22. Parks, *Kirby Smith*, 206–10. Various references to Kirby Smith's mindset during this time can also be found in Noe, *Perryville*.
23. Noe, *Perryville*, 39; Hafendorfer, *Battle of Richmond Kentucky*, 81–105.
24. Parks, *Kirby Smith*, 212.
25. *War of the Rebellion*, vol. 16, part 1, 910; Hafendorfer, *Battle of Richmond Kentucky*, 107–11.
26. *War of the Rebellion*, vol. 16, part 1, 910.
27. Ibid., 945–946; Hafendorfer, *Battle of Richmond Kentucky*, 113–16.
28. *War of the Rebellion*, vol. 16, part 1, 934–35, 945–46.
29. Ibid., 912.
30. *War of the Rebellion*, vol. 16, part 1, 934; Hafendorfer, *Battle of Richmond Kentucky*, 393.
31. Hafendorfer, *Battle of Richmond Kentucky*, 145.
32. *War of the Rebellion*, vol. 16, part 1, 945–46.

33. Ibid., 912–13.

34. Hafendorfer, *Battle of Richmond Kentucky*, 185–97, 232.

35. Ibid., 211–30.

36. Ibid.; see also *War of the Rebellion*, vol. 16, part 1, 908.

37. *War of the Rebellion*, vol. 16, part 1, 908; Hafendorfer, *Battle of Richmond Kentucky*, 232–37.

38. *War of the Rebellion*, vol. 16, part 1, 908; Hafendorfer, *Battle of Richmond Kentucky*, 245–76.

39. Hafendorfer, *Battle of Richmond Kentucky*, 293, 297; see also Noe, *Perryville*, 39.

40. Casualty figures are drawn from Hafendorfer, *Battle of Richmond Kentucky*, 397–402. His research is the most modern on this topic. For a good discussion on the Battle of Second Manassas, see Hennessy, *Return to Bull Run*.

41. Noe, *Perryville*, 40; *War of the Rebellion*, vol. 16, part 1, 933.

42. *War of the Rebellion*, vol. 16, part 1, 933.

Chapter 3

43. McWhiney, *Braxton Bragg*, 274–81; Noe, *Perryville*, 54–58. Until his death in 1864, Polk remained bishop of Louisiana in addition to his military duties.

44. Ibid.

45. Ibid.

46. Daniel, *Days of Glory*, 35, 43–45, 47, 56; Noe, *Perryville*, 10–14.

47. Noe, *Perryville*, 42–48.

48. Ibid., 48–62. Alexander McCook was Robert McCook's younger brother.

49. Ibid.

50. *War of the Rebellion*, vol. 16, part 1, 974, 1089–90.

51. Ibid., 959–61.

52. Ibid., 972–76.

53. Ibid.

54. Ibid.

55. Ibid.; see also 987–88.

56. Ibid., 984–87.

57. Ibid., 961, 982.

58. Ibid., 978–81.

59. Ibid., 965–66. There is some disagreement as to when Dunham took command. He says in his report that it was the morning of September 15, but Chalmers clearly received notes from Dunham in command on the evening of September 14. September 14, 1862, was the date of the Battle of South Mountain in Maryland.

60. Ibid., 964, 1090; see also *Confederate Veteran* 17 (February 1909): 84–85.

61. *War of the Rebellion*, vol. 16, part 1, 965–66, 969–70.

62. Ibid.

63. Ibid., 962, 969–71. The garrison at Harpers Ferry had surrendered over twelve thousand men on September 15, 1862, in the largest capitulation of U.S. forces in the Civil War. In terms of number of men, the Harpers Ferry defeat is surpassed only by the fall of Bataan on April 9, 1942, when seventy-six thousand American and Filipino troops capitulated to the Japanese.

64. Ibid.

65. *Confederate Veteran* 17, 85.

66. Ibid.; see also *War of the Rebellion*, vol. 16, part 1, 970–71.

67. *War of the Rebellion*, vol. 16, part 1, 962; for information about Antietam and casualties, see Murfin, *Gleam of Bayonets*. Wilder's men marched out at 6:00 a.m. Munfordville time (Central Time), which is 7:00 a.m. Maryland time (Eastern Time). By that time, the Battle of Antietam had been underway for about two hours.

68. *War of the Rebellion*, vol. 16, part 1, 968.

69. Daniel, *Days of Glory*, 120–22. Ironically, both armies were using the others' fortifications as part of their defense; the Confederates based their positions around Fort Craig (built by the Federals), while Buell's men used works at Bowling Green originally constructed in 1861 by the Confederates.

70. Ibid., 121–23.

71. The best explanation of Bragg's situation at Munfordville is in McWhiney, *Braxton Bragg*, 286–92. The temperature there on September 16 was around one hundred degrees Fahrenheit. Here is Bragg's summary from his report:

This surrender having been received and completed on September 17, dispositions were made for an attack from General Buell's main force, supposed to be advancing on our rear from Bowling Green. Efforts were made to draw him to an attack by maneuvering a division in his front, while our main force held position south of the intrenchments on Green River. I failed to accomplish this object. With my effective force present, reduced by sickness, exhaustion, and the recent affair before the intrenchments at Munfordville, to half that of the enemy, I could not prudently afford to attack him there in his selected position. Should I pursue him farther toward Bowling Green he might fall back to that place and behind his fortifications. Reduced at the end of four days to three days' rations, and in a hostile country, utterly destitute of supplies, a serious engagement brought on anywhere in that direction could not fail (whatever its results) to materially cripple me. The loss of a battle would be eminently disastrous. I was well aware also that he had a practicable route by way of Morgantown or Brownsville to the Ohio River and thence to Louisville. We were therefore compelled to give up the object and seek for subsistance. Orders were sent for a supply train from our depot at Lexington to meet us in Bardstown, and the march was commenced for the latter place.

Chapter 4

72. Noe, *Perryville*, 82–89; see also Gould and Kennedy, eds., *John Henry Otto*, 19–21.
73. Noe, *Perryville*, 82–89.
74. *War of the Rebellion*, vol. 16, part 1, 892, 957.
75. George Morgan, "Cumberland Gap," in *Battles and Leaders of the Civil War*, eds. Johnson and Buel, 69.
76. Ibid., 61–69; see also Craighill, *Army Officer's Pocket Companion*.
77. *War of the Rebellion*, vol. 16, part 1, 1000.
78. Ibid., 992–93.
79. Ibid., 957–59. Marshall, in reality, had about nine thousand men in his command.
80. Ibid., 957, 992–93; see also Johnson and Buel, *Battles and Leaders of the Civil War*, 61–67.

81. *War of the Rebellion*, vol. 16, part 1, 1004. At the same time, two hundred miles to the west in Munfordville, Chalmers's last attacks against Fort Craig had just been repulsed.
82. Johnson and Buel, *Battles and Leaders of the Civil War*, 66–67.
83. *War of the Rebellion*, vol. 16, part 1, 993–94.
84. Ibid.
85. Ibid.; Johnson and Buel, *Battles and Leaders of the Civil War*, 67–68.
86. Johnson and Buel, *Battles and Leaders of the Civil War*, 67–68.
87. Ibid.
88. *War of the Rebellion*, vol. 16, part 1, 991, 994; Johnson and Buel, *Battles and Leaders of the Civil War*, 67–68.
89. Johnson and Buel, *Battles and Leaders of the Civil War*, 68.
90. *War of the Rebellion*, vol. 16, part 2, 850–52; Parks, *Kirby Smith*, 227–28.
91. Ibid.
92. *War of the Rebellion*, vol. 16, part 1, 994–95; Johnson and Buel, *Battles and Leaders of the Civil War*, 68–69.
93. Johnson and Buel, *Battles and Leaders of the Civil War*, 68–69.
94. Ibid.
95. *War of the Rebellion*, vol. 16, part 1, 995–96; Johnson and Buel, *Battles and Leaders of the Civil War*, 27–28, 68–69.
96. Ibid. Additional information on the 6th Tennessee's action can be found in *War of the Rebellion*, vol. 16, part 2, 558–59.
97. Ibid.

Chapter 5

98. John Inglis Diary, typescript at PBSHS; Daniel Adams, letter of September 23, 1862, typescript at PBSHS.
99. Ibid.
100. Noe, *Perryville*, 99–100.
101. Ibid., 99–101; Harrison, *Civil War in Kentucky*, 47–48.
102. Noe, *Perryville*, 99–103; Harrison, *Civil War in Kentucky*, 34–35, 47–48.
103. Ibid.; McWhiney, *Braxton Bragg*, 297–99; for Bragg's message, see *War of the Rebellion*, vol. 16, part 2, 876. The emphasis is in the original.
104. Noe, *Perryville*, 103–04; McWhiney, *Braxton Bragg*, 298–99.

105. Noe, *Perryville*, 89–92.

106. *War of the Rebellion*, vol. 16, part 2, 538, 554–55.

107. Ibid.

108. Noe, *Perryville*, 92–98.

109. Ibid.

110. Ibid.

111. Ibid.; *War of the Rebellion*, vol. 16, part 2, 558–59.

112. Noe, *Perryville*, 92–98. I Corps later became XX Corps in 1863.

113. Ibid. Crittenden Drive in Louisville (outside Churchill Downs) is named for the family. II Corps later became XXI Corps in 1863.

114. Ibid. III Corps became XIV Corps in 1863.

115. Ibid.

116. Ibid.; *War of the Rebellion*, vol. 16, part 1, 184.

117. McWhiney, *Braxton Bragg*, 297–301. Hawes had been inaugurated as governor earlier in 1862 after his predecessor George Johnson was killed at Shiloh. The ceremony that Bragg planned was properly termed an installation.

Chapter 6

118. Noe, *Perryville*, 111–12.

119. Pendergast, *Pen Pictures from the 2nd Minnesota*, 24–25.

120. McWhiney, *Braxton Bragg*, 299–300; *War of the Rebellion*, vol. 16, part 2, 895–98.

121. *War of the Rebellion*, vol. 16, part 2, 895–98.

122. *War of the Rebellion*, vol. 16, part 1, 1100–102; *War of the Rebellion*, vol. 16, part 2, 901.

123. Fitch, *Echoes of the Civil War*, 55–56.

124. Ibid.

125. *War of the Rebellion*, vol. 16, part 2, 901.

126. *War of the Rebellion*, vol. 16, part 1, 1019; *War of the Rebellion*, vol. 16, part 2, 904.

127. *War of the Rebellion*, vol. 16, part 2, 904; Parks, *Kirby Smith*, 233.

128. Today the Old State Capitol in Frankfort.

129. Harrison, *Civil War in Kentucky*, 48–49; Noe, *Perryville*, 129.

130. Ibid.; see also *War of the Rebellion*, vol. 16, part 1, 1020. Hawes's government never returned to Frankfort and spent the rest of the war in exile.
131. Noe, *Perryville*, 114.
132. *War of the Rebellion*, vol. 16, part 1, 1091–92.
133. Pendergast, *Pen Pictures from the 2nd Minnesota*, 24.
134. Noe, *Perryville*, 120–24; the quotes come from Beatty, *Citizen Soldier*.
135. *War of the Rebellion*, vol. 16, part 1, 1024–25, 1096; Joseph Wheeler, "Bragg's Invasion of Kentucky," in *Battles and Leaders of the Civil War*, eds. Johnson and Buel, 4–6; see also Wheeler's battle report, typescript in PBSHS files.
136. *War of the Rebellion*, vol. 16, part 1, 1025.
137. Noe, *Perryville*, 187–88.

Chapter 7

138. This and the preceding paragraphs are constructed using the information files and archive at the Perryville Enhancement Project, Perryville, KY. See also Harmon, *Chaplin Hills*, and Noe, *Perryville*, 107–12. Kentucky State Park today commemorates this area's significant state history with Old Fort Harrod State Park (Harrodsburg), Constitution Square State Historic Site (Danville) and Isaac Shelby State Historic Site (Danville). Perryville Battlefield is also a State Historic Site.
139. Ibid.
140. *War of the Rebellion*, vol. 16, part 1, 1119–20, 1157–58.
141. Ibid., 1081.
142. Stewart, *McCook's Regiment*, 1–26.
143. *War of the Rebellion*, vol. 16, part 1, 1085; Stewart, *McCook's Regiment*, 26–27; see also Beaudot, *24th Wisconsin*, 89–90.
144. Beaudot, *24th Wisconsin*, 89–93; for background on Arthur and Douglas MacArthur, see Manchester, *American Caesar*, and MacArthur, *Reminiscences*.
145. *War of the Rebellion*, vol. 16, part 1, 1158.
146. Beaudot, *24th Wisconsin*, 91–92.
147. Johnson and Buel, *Battles and Leaders of the Civil War*, 52–53; Noe, *Perryville*, 157–59.

148. Noe, *Perryville*, 372, 379–80.

149. *War of the Rebellion*, vol. 16, part 1, 1109–10.

150. Ibid., 1025.

151. Johnson and Buel, *Battles and Leaders of the Civil War*, 16–18.

152. Gould and Kennedy, *John Henry Otto*, 42–44.

153. For a discussion of Rousseau's division and Starkweather's brigade in particular, see Kolakowski, "John C. Starkweather at Perryville," 93–117; see also the John C. Russell War Claim, typescript in PBSHS.

154. Kolakowski, "John C. Starkweather at Perryville," 104–05. The 2nd and 33rd Ohio both contained men who had been part of the famous Andrews Raid (Great Locomotive Chase) the previous spring and had successfully escaped back to Union lines.

155. Ibid.

156. *War of the Rebellion*, vol. 16, part 1, 1087, 1092–93.

157. Kolakowski, "John C. Starkweather at Perryville," 105.

158. Ibid.

159. Lambert, *Heroes of the Western Theater*, 127–129. See also Noe, *Perryville*, 144–88.

160. *War of the Rebellion*, vol. 16, part 1, 1110–11.

Chapter 8

161. John C. Starkweather, letter to the *National Tribune*, November 4, 1886 (hereafter cited as "Starkweather report"). See also Kolakowski, "John C. Starkweather at Perryville."

162. Ibid.; Gould and Kennedy, *John Henry Otto*, 45–46; Fitch, *Echoes of the Civil War*, 58–59.

163. *War of the Rebellion*, vol. 16, part 1, 1045; Fitch, *Echoes of the Civil War*, 58–59.

164. Noe, *Perryville*, 195–96.

165. Kolakowski, "John C. Starkweather at Perryville," 107; unsigned, "History of the 16th Tennessee Infantry," typescript in PBSHS.

166. Kolakowski, "John C. Starkweather at Perryville," 107; Thomas R. Hooper diary, PBSHS; Widow Gibson File, PBSHS.

167. Kolakowski, "John C. Starkweather at Perryville," 107; see also Noe, *Perryville*. Recent deed research by the Perryville Enhancement Project shows that the fence marks a property line laid down in the 1790s.
168. *War of the Rebellion*, vol. 16, part 1, 1060, 1156–57.
169. *War of the Rebellion*, vol. 16, part 1, 1114–15.
170. Noe, *Perryville*, 209; *War of the Rebellion*, vol. 16, part 1, 1060.
171. Noe, *Perryville*, 209.
172. *War of the Rebellion*, vol. 16, part 1, 1115; Thomas H. Malone Memoir, PBSHS; Josiah Ayre Diary, typescript in PBSHS.
173. Malone Memoir, PBSHS; Noe, *Perryville*, 210–13; Kolakowski, "John C. Starkweather at Perryville," 107.
174. Kolakowski, "John C. Starkweather at Perryville," 99, 108; James Pillar letter, undated typescript, PBSHS.
175. Kolakowski, "John C. Starkweather at Perryville," 108; Pillar letter, PBSHS; Noe, *Perryville*, 251.
176. Pillar letter, PBSHS; Charles W. Carr letters, *Wisconsin Magazine of History* 43 (Summer 1960), letter of October 10, 1862; see also Kolakowski, "John C. Starkweather at Perryville," 108–09.
177. Kolakowski, "John C. Starkweather at Perryville," 109.
178. Elias Hoover, letter to the *National Tribune*, June 20, 1889. The 1st Wisconsin was based on militia units from Madison and Milwaukee, and today is part of the Wisconsin National Guard as the 127th Infantry Regiment.
179. Gould and Kennedy, *John Henry Otto*, 48; William S. Mitchell letters, typescript in PBSHS. The emphasis is in the original.
180. *War of the Rebellion*, vol. 16, part 1, 1113–14, 1155–56.

Chapter 9

181. Noe, *Perryville*, 215–17; *War of the Rebellion*, vol. 16, part 1, 1120–21; Thomas Jones Biography typescript, PBSHS.
182. *War of the Rebellion*, vol. 16, part 1, 1049.
183. Dr. George Little and James Maxwell, *A History of Lumsden's Battery CSA* (Tuscaloosa, AL: UDC, n.d.), 5, typescript in PBSHS; Darrell Young and Kurt Holman, various conversations with the author.

184. Noe, *Perryville*, 217; Robert A. Jarman manuscript, typescript in PBSHS.

185. Angus Waddle quoted in *Heroes of the Western Theater*, Lambert, 127; Landt, *Your Country Calls*, 40.

186. Noe, *Perryville*, 218; John Freeman Diary, October 8, 1862, typescript in PBSHS.

187. John Inglis Diary, October 8, 1862, PBSHS.

188. Ibid.; William Miller report, typescript in PBSHS.

189. Landt, *Your Country Calls*, 40.

190. William Miller Report, PBSHS; *War of the Rebellion*, vol. 16, part 1, 1050.

191. *War of the Rebellion*, vol. 16, part 1, 1120–21; see also Buckner's manuscript report, typescript at PBSHS.

192. *War of the Rebellion*, vol. 16, part 1, 1125; Noe, *Perryville*, 219–24. General Johnson had celebrated his forty-fifth birthday only the day before.

193. *War of the Rebellion*, vol. 16, part 1, 1133; Noe, *Perryville*, 219–24.

194. Ibid.

195. Ibid.

196. Beatty, *Citizen Soldier*, 178; Noe, *Perryville*, 224–25; *War of the Rebellion*, vol. 16, part 1, 1132.

197. *War of the Rebellion*, vol. 52, part 1, 51–53.

198. Noe, *Perryville*, 373; see William P. McDowell, *The History of the 15th Kentucky Infantry* (undated), PBSHS. The best study on the 15th Kentucky is Kirk Jenkins's excellent book, *The Battle Rages Higher*. In this battle for the control of the state, the 15th was the only large Kentucky unit engaged on either side. Although Kentucky units were present in II and III Corps and the Confederate cavalry, only the 15th and a few artillery batteries saw major action on October 8.

199. Buckner's report, PBSHS; *War of the Rebellion*, vol. 16, part 1, 1122–23.

200. Beatty, *Citizen Soldier*, 179.

201. *War of the Rebellion*, vol. 16, part 1, 1047, 1123; *War of the Rebellion*, vol. 52, part 1, 51–53.

202. *War of the Rebellion*, vol. 16, part 1, 1050.

Chapter 10

203. Johnson and Buel, *Battles and Leaders of the Civil War*, 48; John M. Harlan letter, University of Louisville.

204. *War of the Rebellion*, vol. 16, part 1, 1022.

205. Author conversations with Kurt Holman and Darrell Young, PBSHS.

206. Starkweather Report; Elias Hoover, *National Tribune*, June 20, 1889.

207. Starkweather Report; Fitch, *Echoes of the Civil War*, 60–61; Gould and Kennedy, *John Henry Otto*, 48–49; *War of the Rebellion*, vol. 16, part I, 1040.

208. Noe, *Perryville*, 258–63.

209. Gould and Kennedy, *John Henry Otto*, 49; Noe, *Perryville*, 260–261; author's conversations with Kurt Holman and Darrell Young, PBSHS; Theodore Herrling, *National Tribune*, August 26, 1886. Amateur archaeologists would later discover the greatest concentration of shot and shell on this part of the battlefield.

210. Starkweather Report; John Durham and Morris Rice's accounts come from an undated typescript, PBSHS; see also Elias Hoover, *National Tribune*, June 20, 1889. A close reading of Starkweather's report shows the sequence of events given here, and McCook's report specifically speaks of Starkweather "routing" the Confederates. Other Federal accounts also refer to an advance back to the first position. There is some debate as to the identity of the flag the 1st Wisconsin captured at Perryville. Most Federal sources identify it as the 1st Tennessee's flag, but the Tennesseans insist that they did not lose a flag at Perryville. As far as can be ascertained, the other regiments of Maney's brigade also carried their colors safely off the field. The sole exception in the documentation is the 27th Tennessee, which lost so many men at this battle that very few accounts exist of its actions. Because of its heavy losses, the 1st and 27th were consolidated in the late fall of 1862.

211. *War of the Rebellion*, vol. 16, part 1, 1066.

212. *War of the Rebellion*, vol. 52, part 1, 51–53.

213. Ibid.; see also *War of the Rebellion*, vol. 16, part 1, 1067–68; see also Hoffman, *My Brave Mechanics*, 107–8.

214. *War of the Rebellion*, vol. 52, part 1, 51–53.

215. Author unknown, typescript of 33rd Alabama Company B in PBSHS.

216. Johnson and Buel, *Battles and Leaders of the Civil War*, 61; *War of the Rebellion*, vol. 16, part 1, 1079–80.

217. *War of the Rebellion*, vol. 16, part 1, 1079–80; Mayfield, "Hoosier Invades the Confederacy," copy in PBSHS, 149–50. Gooding's command also included the rookie 74th Illinois, but that regiment was detached before the battle to guard wagons.

218. 33rd Alabama Co. B typescript, PBSHS; *War of the Rebellion*, vol. 16, part 1, 1080, 1159.

219. *War of the Rebellion*, vol. 16, part 1, 1080, 1159; Mayfield, "Hoosier Invades the Confederacy," 149–50.

220. This and the preceding paragraph are constructed using *War of the Rebellion*, vol. 16, part 1, 1159; *Confederate Veteran* 7, 549–50; and Noe, *Perryville*, 301–2.

221. Ibid.; Mayfield, "Hoosier Invades the Confederacy," 150.

222. *War of the Rebellion*, vol. 16, part 1, 1080–81, 1159–60; Noe, *Perryville*, 301–5. Steedman's brigade arrived in the Dixville Crossroads area about 6:00 p.m. but had been held in reserve by McCook. The brigade finally advanced with a cheer about 7:00 p.m.

223. Noe, *Perryville*, 277–92. See also the Perryville Street Fighting File in the archives of the Perryville Enhancement Project.

224. Ibid. The Masonic hall was one of the buildings that caught fire and burned down. The local Masonic lodge, Harvey Maguire #209, is the only lodge in Kentucky to have its charter destroyed in battle.

225. Ibid.; Harlan letter, UL.

226. Noe, *Perryville*, 369, 373; *War of the Rebellion*, vol. 16, part 1, 1087.

Chapter 11

227. Noe, *Perryville*, 373; for details on this meeting see Daniel, *Days of Glory*, 158–59.

228. Noe, *Perryville*, 369; *War of the Rebellion*, vol. 16, part 1, 1093.

229. Pendergast, *Pen Pictures from the 2nd Minnesota*, 26; 33rd Alabama Co. B typescript, PBSHS.

230. Daniel, *Days of Glory*, 158.

231. Parks, *Kirby Smith*, 234–35; *War of the Rebellion*, vol. 16, part 1, 1135–36.

232. Parks, *Kirby Smith*, 237.

233. Daniel, *Days of Glory*, 167.

234. Parks, *Kirby Smith*, 237–38.

235. McWhiney, *Braxton Bragg*, 320–22; *War of the Rebellion*, vol. 16, part 1, 1088.

236. Ibid.

237. Daniel, *Days of Glory*, 168–73.

238. Davis, *Orphan Brigade*, 135–36.

239. Ibid.

240. Daniel, *Days of Glory*, 173–77; *War of the Rebellion*, vol. 16, part 1, 11–12.

241. A.N. Read Report, typescript in PBSHS. H.P. Bottom was a self-sufficient farmer before October 8, 1862; after that date, he had to buy food for his family for the rest of his life.

242. J.J. Polk Memoir, typescript in Perryville Enhancement Project Archives; Casualty Database, PBSHS. The battle also permanently altered Perryville's geography: in the 1870s, the city's streets were renamed for Union and Confederate generals.

Appendix II

243. *War of the Rebellion*, vol. 16, part 1, 124–25.

244. Steedman was premature to call Fry a division commander in late October 1862. Fry was later promoted and was commanding a division when this testimony was given in December 1862.

245. Ibid., 134–36.

246. Ibid., 221–22.

247. John M. Harlan, undated typescript, John Marshall Harlan Papers, University of Louisville. Paragraph spacing was added for ease of reading.

BIBLIOGRAPHY

Books

Beatty, John. *The Citizen Soldier*. Cincinnati, OH: Wilstach, Baldwin & Co., 1879.

Beaudot, William J.K. *The 24th Wisconsin in the Civil War: The Biography of a Regiment*. Mechanicsburg, PA: Stackpole, 2003.

Catton, Bruce. *Grant Moves South*. Boston: Little, Brown, 1960.

Craighill, William P. *The Army Officer's Pocket Companion*. New York: Van Nostrand, 1862.

Daniel, Larry. *Days of Glory: The Army of the Cumberland*. Baton Rouge: Louisiana State University Press, 2004.

Davis, William C. *The Orphan Brigade*. Baton Rouge: Louisiana State University Press, 1980.

Fitch, Michael H. *Echoes of the Civil War as I Hear Them*. New York: R.F. Fenno, 1905.

Gould, David, and James P. Kennedy, eds. *Memoirs of a Dutch Mudsill: The War Memories of John Henry Otto*. Kent, OH: Kent State University Press, 2004.

BIBLIOGRAPHY

Hafendorfer, Kenneth. *The Battle of Richmond Kentucky.* Louisville, KY: K.H. Press, 2006.

Harmon, Geraldine C. *Chaplin Hills.* Danville, KY: Bluegrass Printing, 1971.

Harrison, Lowell. *The Civil War in Kentucky.* Lexington: University Press of Kentucky, 1975.

Hennessy, John. *Return to Bull Run.* New York: Simon & Schuster, 1993.

Hoffman, Mark. *My Brave Mechanics: The First Michigan Engineers and Their Civil War.* Detroit, MI: Wayne State University Press, 2007.

Jenkins, Kirk. *The Battle Rages Higher.* Lexington: University Press of Kentucky, 2003.

Johnson, Robert Underwood, and Clarence Clough Buel, eds. *Battles and Leaders of the Civil War Volume 3.* New York: Century Company, 1887.

Lambert, Lois J. *Heroes of the Western Theater: 33rd Ohio Veteran Volunteer Infantry.* Milford, OH: Little Miami, 2008.

Landt, Sophronius. *Your Country Calls.* Green Lake, WI: New Past, 2003.

MacArthur, Douglas. *Reminiscences.* New York: Fawcett, 1965.

Manchester, William. *American Caesar.* Boston: Little, Brown, 1978.

McWhiney, Grady. *Braxton Bragg and Confederate Defeat Volume 1: Field Command.* New York: Columbia University Press, 1969.

Murfin, James V. *The Gleam of Bayonets.* Baton Rouge: Louisiana State University Press, 2004.

Noe, Kenneth. *Perryville: This Grand Havoc of Battle.* Lexington: University Press of Kentucky, 2002.

Parks, Joseph H. *General Edmund Kirby Smith CSA*. Baton Rouge: Louisiana State University Press, 1982.

Pendergast, Timothy. *Pen Pictures from the 2ⁿᵈ Minnesota*. Roseville, MN: PGB, 1998.

Richardson, H. Edward. *Cassius Marcellus Clay: Firebrand of Freedom*. Lexington: University Press of Kentucky, 1976.

Stewart, Nixon B. *Dan McCook's Regiment: 52ⁿᵈ O.V.I.* Alliance, OH: Review, 1900.

U.S. War Department. *The War of the Rebellion: A Compilation of the Official Records of the Union and Confederate Armies*. 128 vols. Washington, D.C.: Government Printing Office, 1890–1901.

Articles

Carr, Charles W. "Letters from the 21st Wisconsin." *Wisconsin Magazine of History* 43 (Summer 1960).

Kolakowski, Christopher L. "Magnificent Fighting: John C. Starkweather at Perryville." *New Yorkers in the Civil War* 9 (October 2007).

Mayfield, Leroy S. "A Hoosier Invades the Confederacy." *Indiana Magazine of History* (n.d.).

Periodicals

Confederate Veteran
National Tribune

Unpublished Primary Sources

Perryville Battlefield State Historic Site Collections. Daniel Adams Letter.
————. Josiah Ayre Diary.
————. H.P. Bottom War Claim.
————. O.H. Browning Letter.
————. Simon Bolivar Buckner Report.
————. John Freeman Diary.
————. Widow Gibson File.
————. History of the 15ᵗʰ Kentucky Infantry Manuscript.
————. History of Lumsden's Battery Manuscript.
————. History of 16ᵗʰ Tennessee Infantry Manuscript.
————. Thomas R. Hooper Diary.
————. John Inglis Diary.
————. Robert A. Jarman Manuscript.
————. Thomas Jones Biography.
————. Thomas H. Malone Memoir.
————. William Miller Report.
————. William S. Mitchell Letters.
————. James Pillar Letter.
————. A.N. Read Report.
————. John C. Russell War Claim.
————. 33ʳᵈ Alabama Company B Typescript.

Perryville Enhancement Project Collections

University of Louisville Special Collections. John M. Harlan Papers.

About the Author

C hristopher L. Kolakowski was born and raised in Fredericksburg, Virginia. He received his BA in history and mass communications from Emory & Henry College, and his MA in public history from the State University of New York at Albany. Chris has spent his career interpreting and preserving American military history with the National Park Service, New York State government, the Rensselaer County (New York) Historical Society and the Civil War Preservation Trust. He has written and spoken on the Civil War, American Revolution, Napoleonic Wars and both World Wars. From 2005 to 2008, Chris was executive director of the Perryville Enhancement Project; during his tenure he added 152 acres of critical battlefield land and increased Perryville's national profile. Today, Chris works as a military historian in Atlanta, Georgia. *The Civil War at Perryville: Battling for the Bluegrass State* is his first book.

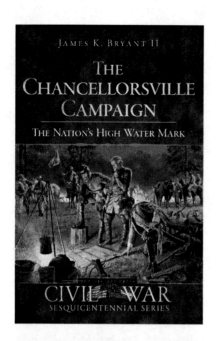

JAMES K. BRYANT II

THE CHANCELLORSVILLE CAMPAIGN

THE NATION'S HIGH WATER MARK

CIVIL WAR
SESQUICENTENNIAL SERIES

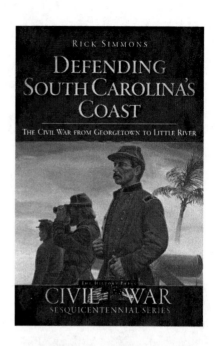

RICK SIMMONS

DEFENDING SOUTH CAROLINA'S COAST

THE CIVIL WAR FROM GEORGETOWN TO LITTLE RIVER

CIVIL WAR
SESQUICENTENNIAL SERIES

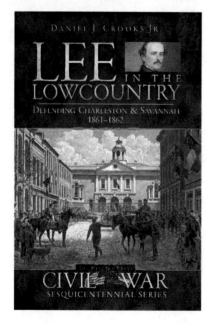

DANIEL J. CROOKS JR.

LEE IN THE LOWCOUNTRY

DEFENDING CHARLESTON & SAVANNAH 1861–1862

CIVIL WAR
SESQUICENTENNIAL SERIES

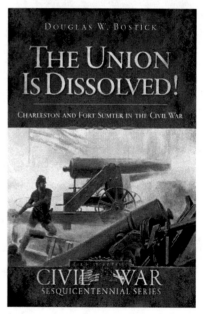

DOUGLAS W. BOSTICK

THE UNION IS DISSOLVED!

CHARLESTON AND FORT SUMTER IN THE CIVIL WAR

CIVIL WAR
SESQUICENTENNIAL SERIES

THE HISTORY PRESS
CIVIL WAR
SESQUICENTENNIAL SERIES

The History Press Civil War Sesquicentennial Series offers thoroughly researched, accessible accounts of important aspects of the war rarely covered outside the academic realm. Explore a range of topics from influential but lesser-known battles and campaigns to the local and regional impact of the war's figures—whether celebrated generals or common soldiers. Each book is crafted in a way that Civil War enthusiasts and casual readers alike will enjoy.

Books in this series from The History Press include:

The Chancellorsville Campaign
978.1.59629.594.0 * 6 x 9 * 160pp * $19.99

Defending South Carolina's Coast
978.1.59629.780.7 * 6 x 9 * 192pp * $21.99

Lee in the Lowcountry
978.1.59629.589.6 * 6 x 9 * 128pp * $19.99

The Union Is Dissolved!
978.1.59629.573.5 * 6 x 9 * 128pp * $19.99

Visit us at
www.historypress.net